Real World Colouring Book

For Advanced Users & Adults

50 Images

Created From Real Life Photos For You To Colour As You Please.

ISBN 978-0-359-82516-5
90000

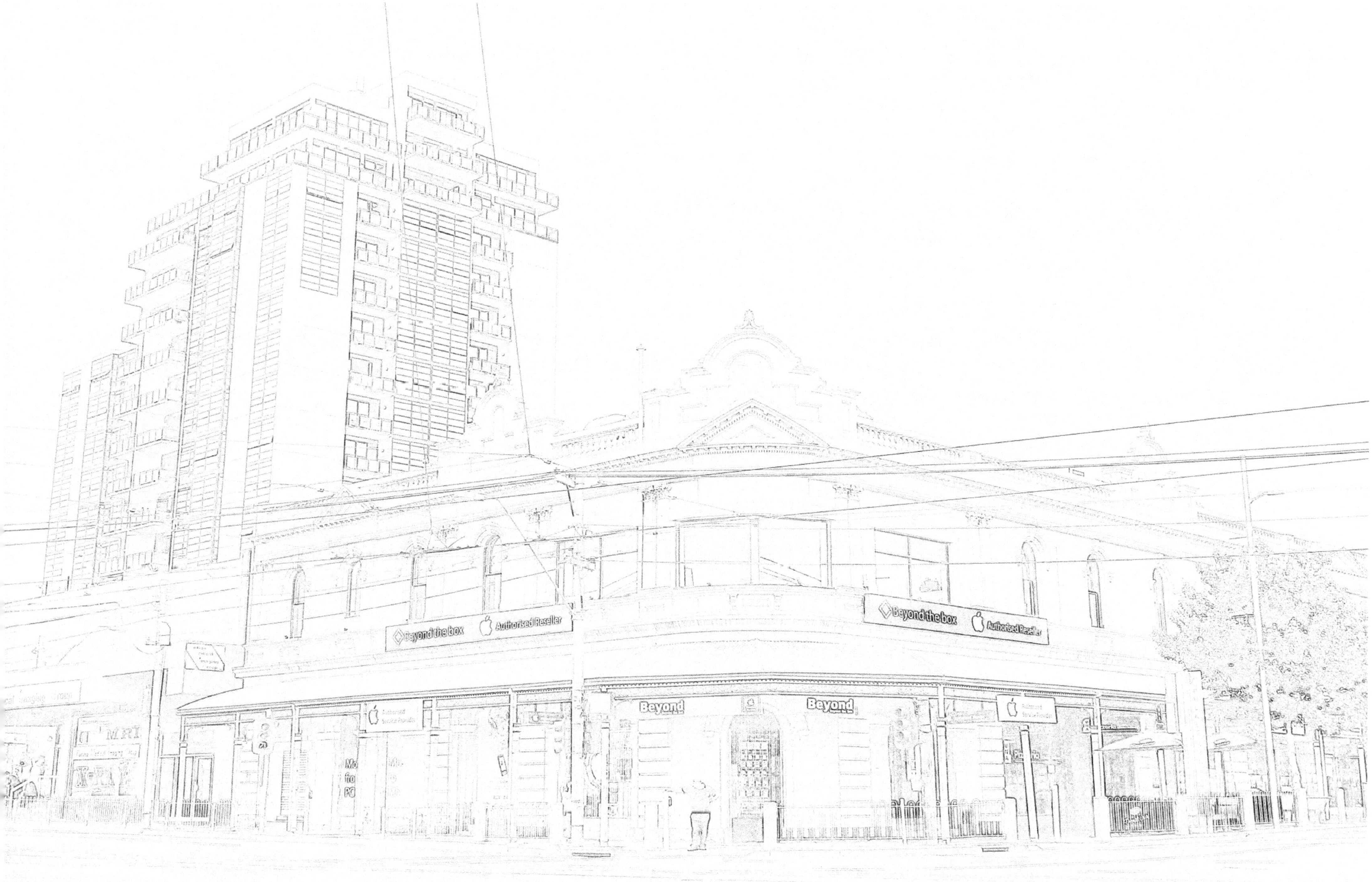
Beyond the box
Authorised Reseller
Beyond the box
Authorised Reseller
Beyond
Beyond
MRI

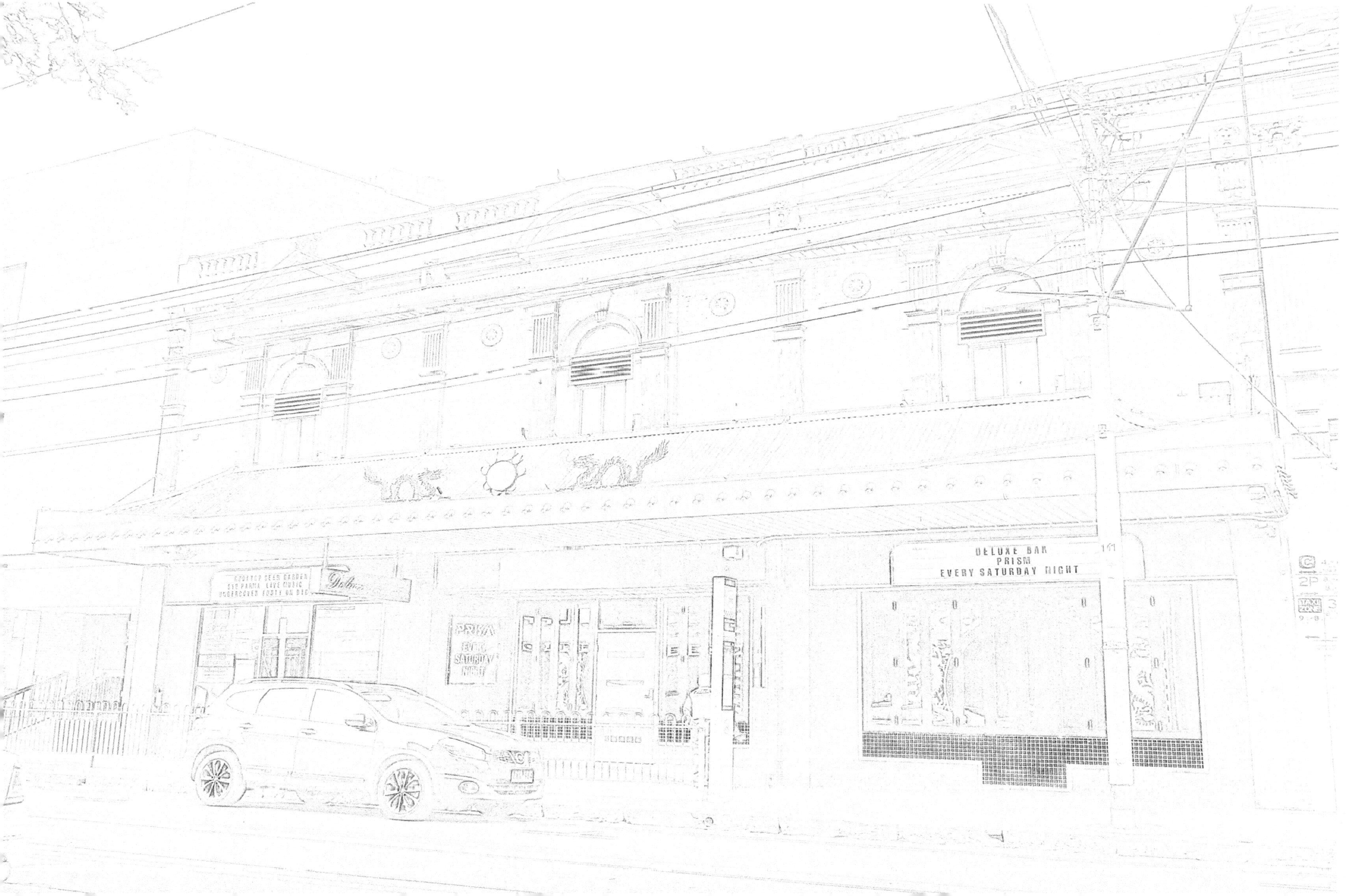
DELUXE BAR
PRISM
EVERY SATURDAY NIGHT
2P
TAXI ZONE

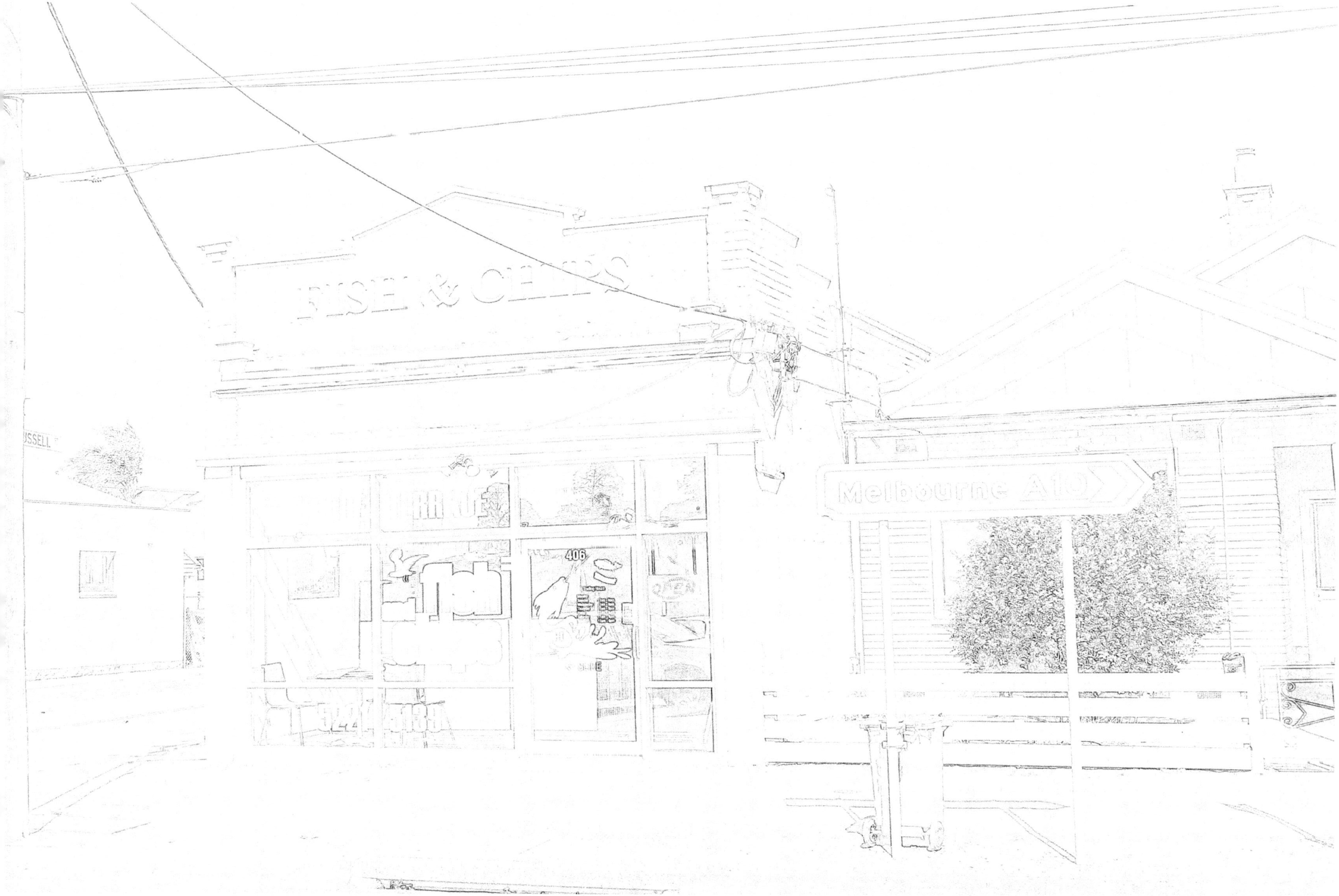
FISH & CHIPS
406
fish
Melbourne A10
USSELL

410

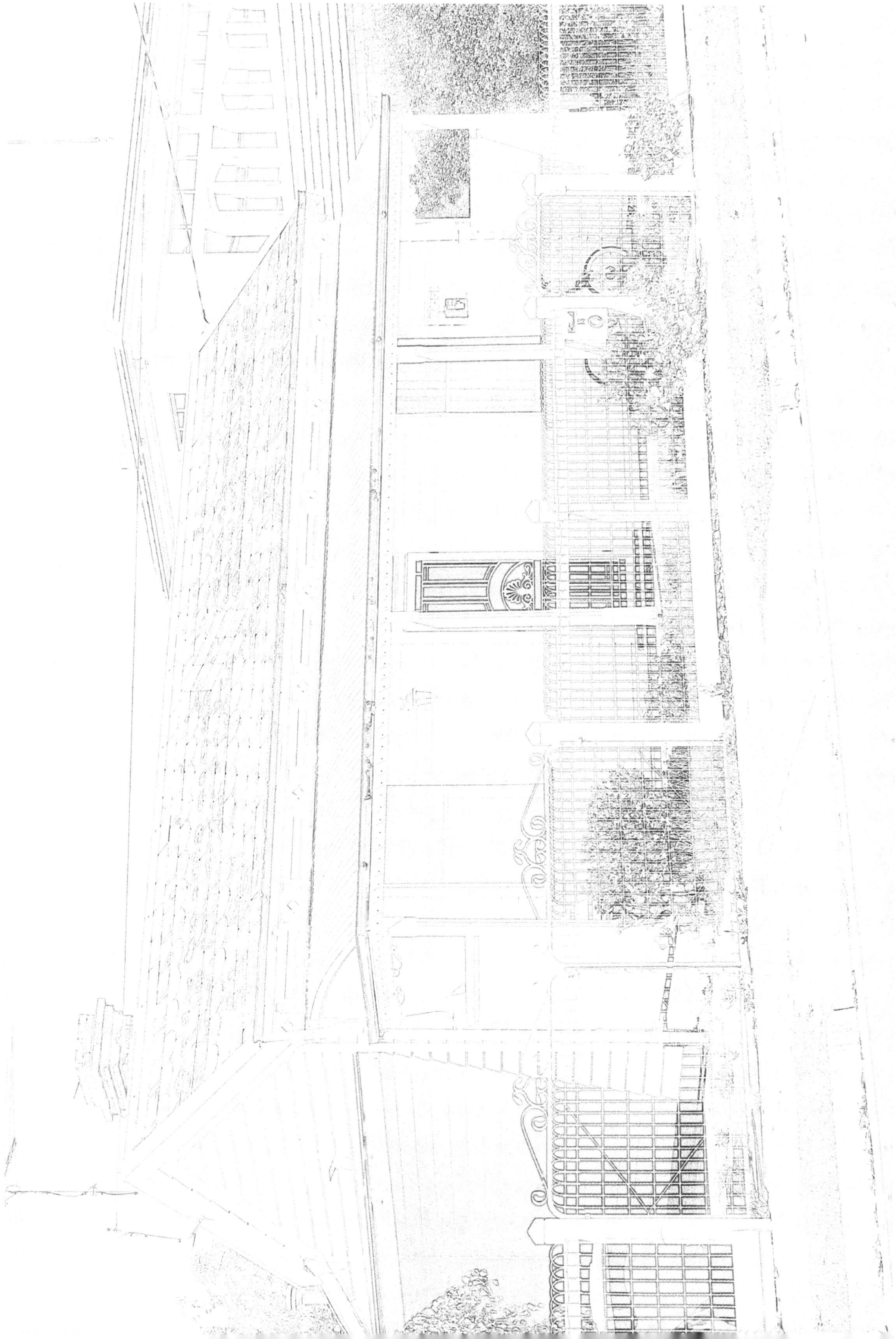

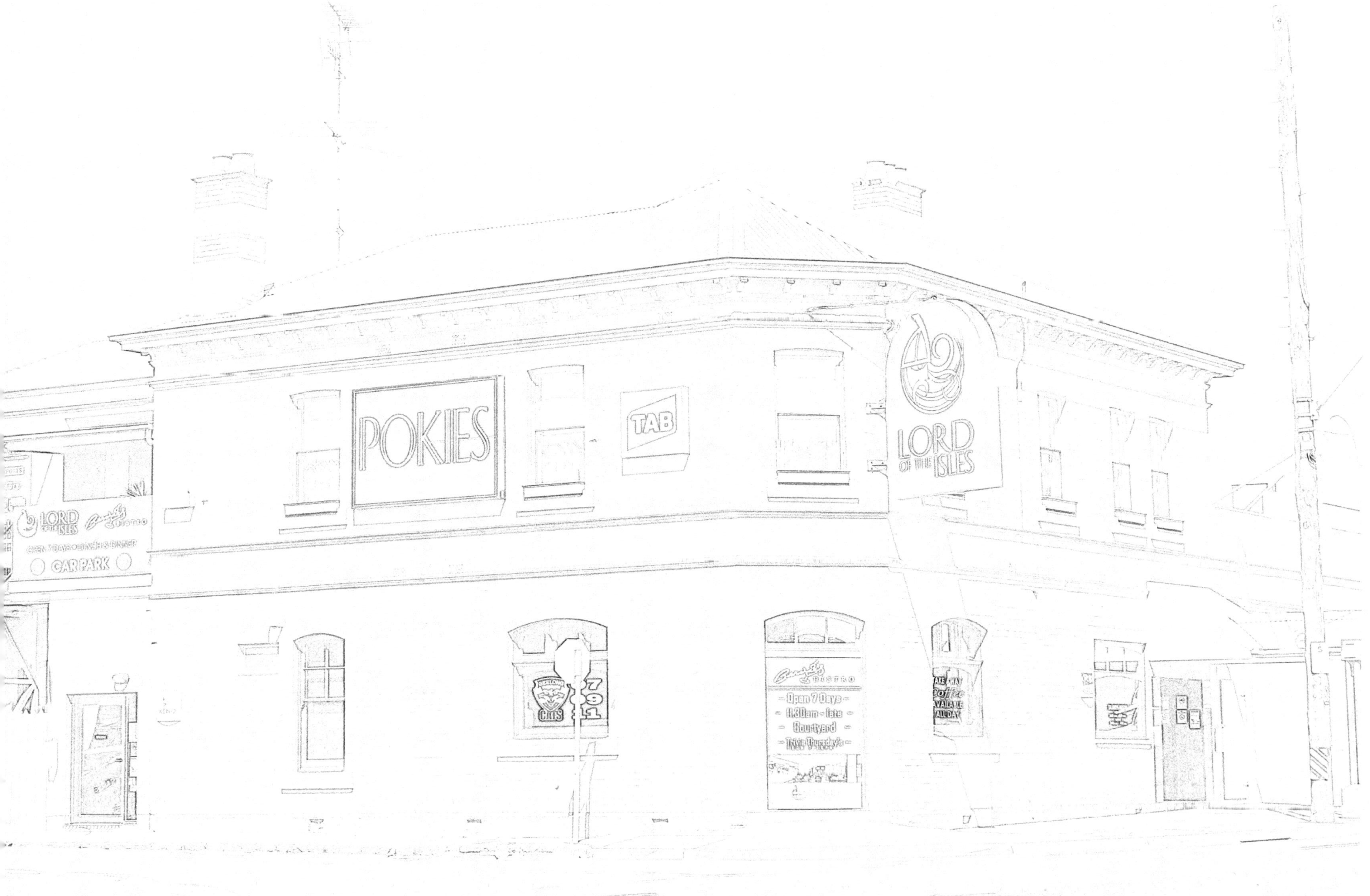
POKIES
TAB
LORD OF THE ISLES
LORD OF THE ISLES
OPEN 7 DAYS LUNCH & DINNER
CAR PARK
BISTRO
Open 7 Days
11.30am - late
Courtyard
Trivia Thursday's
TAKE AWAY
coffee
AVAILABLE
ALL DAY
CATS

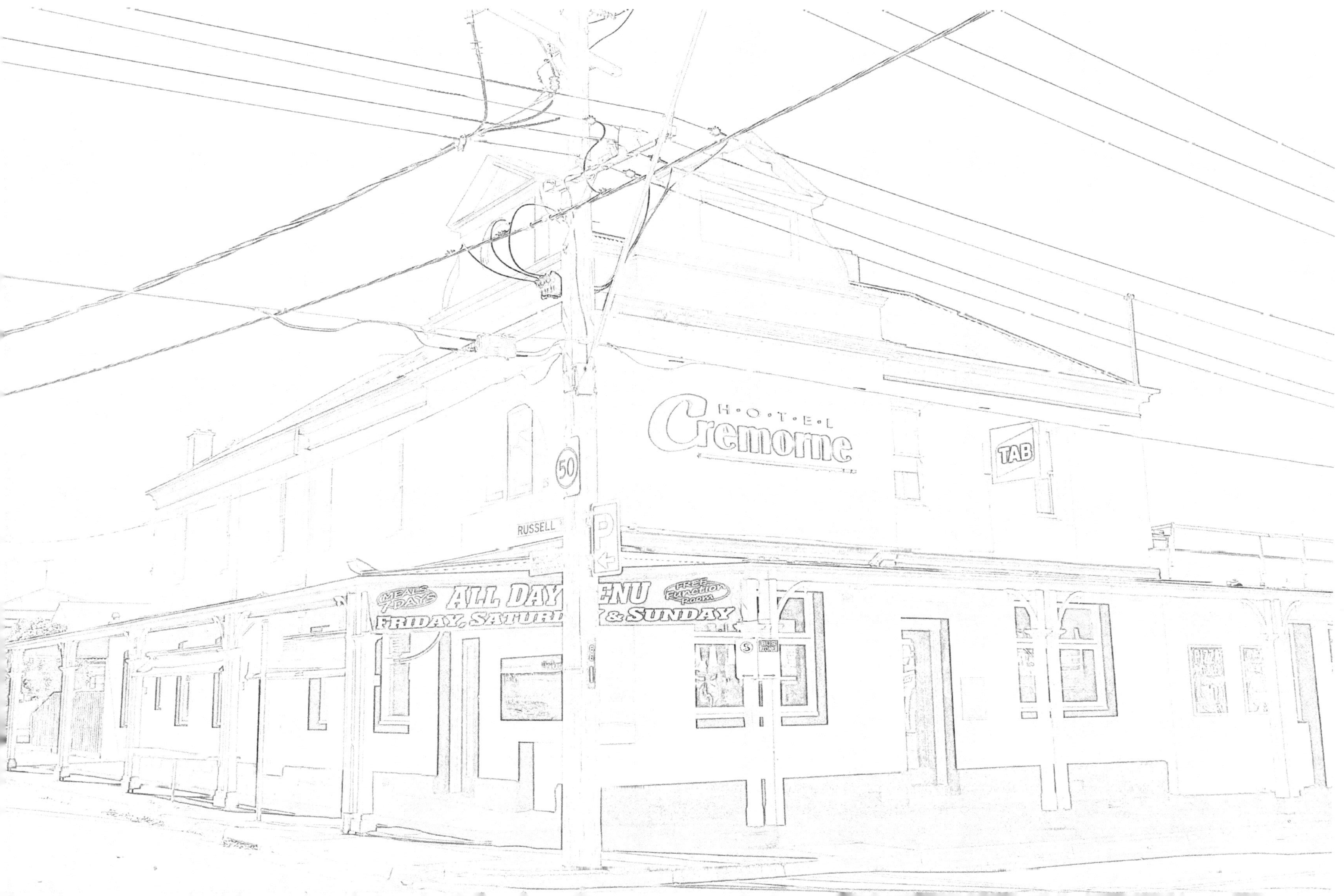
HOTEL
Cremorne
TAB
50
RUSSELL
P
MEALS 7-DAYS
FREE Function Room
& SUNDAY

4/321
millinery
jewellery

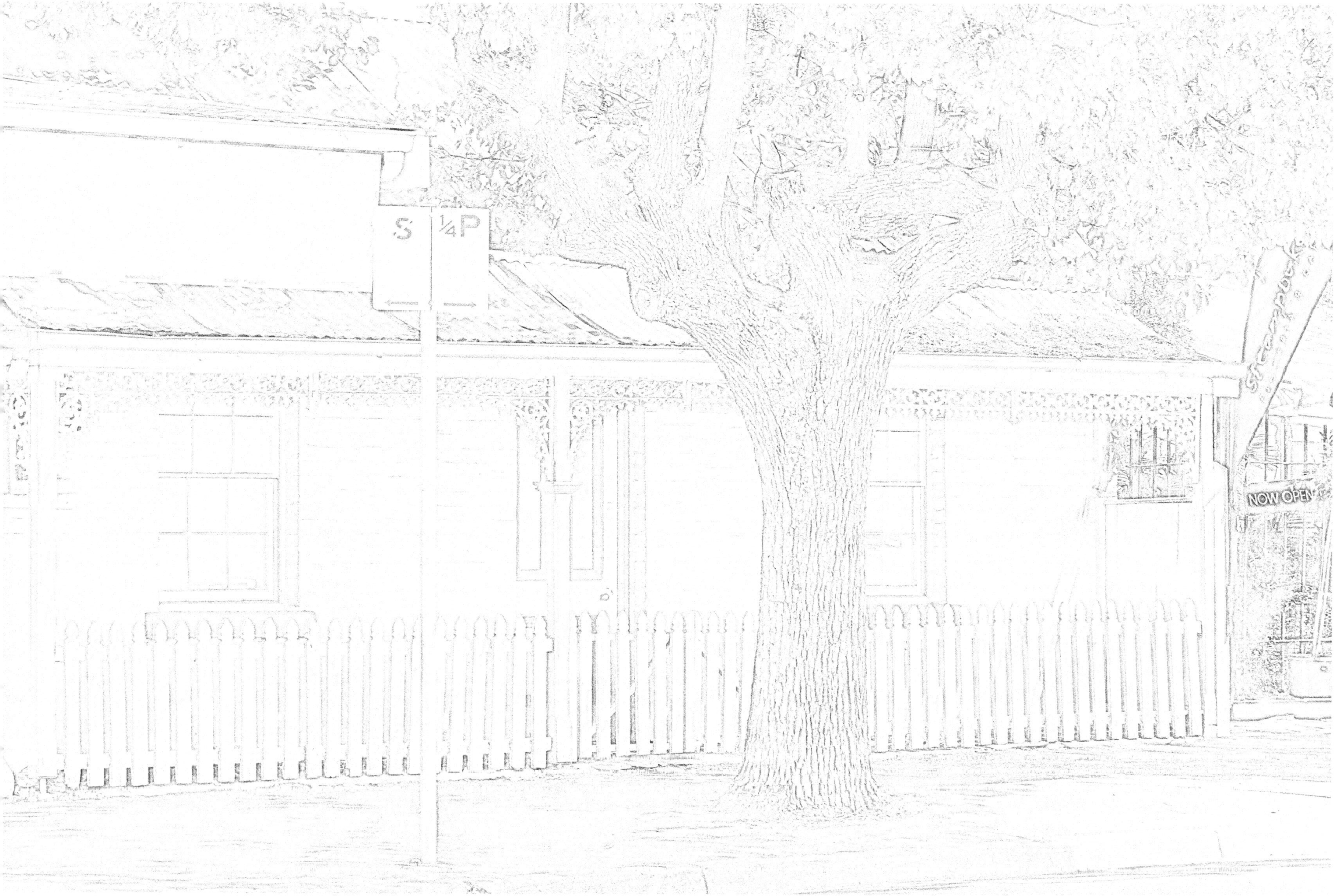
¼P
NOW OPEN

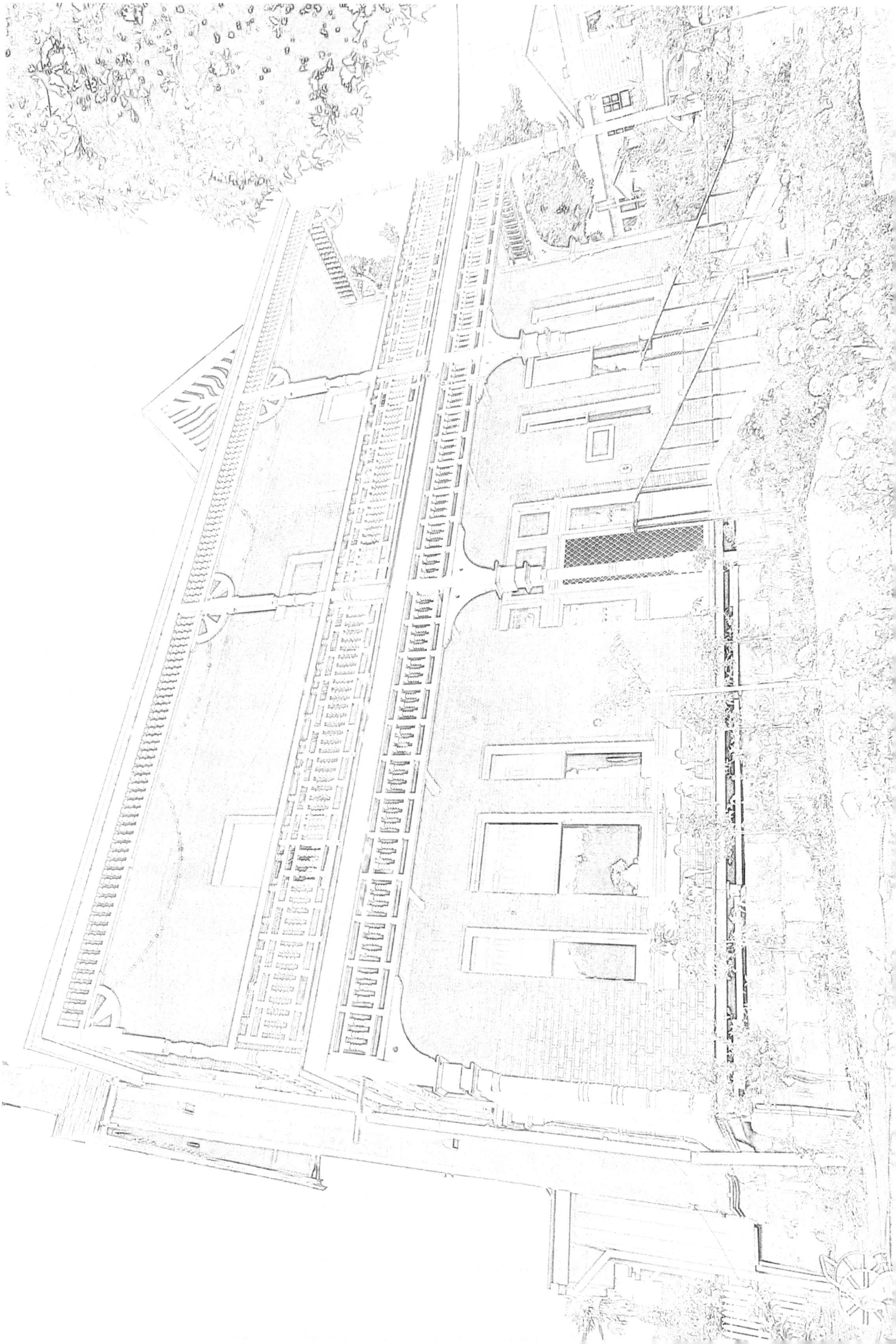

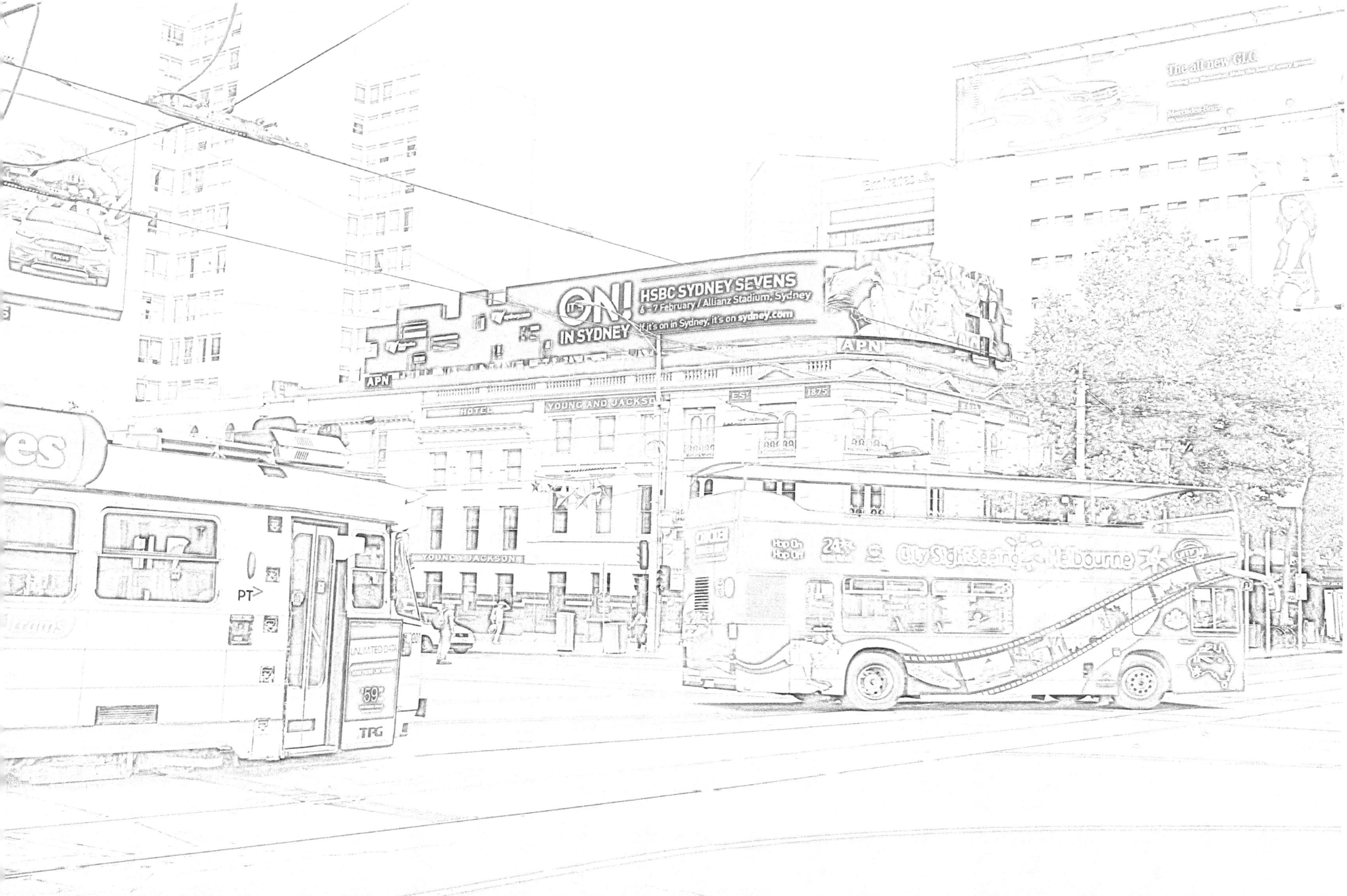

IT'S ON! IN SYDNEY
HSBC SYDNEY SEVENS
6 - 7 February / Allianz Stadium, Sydney
If it's on in Sydney, it's on sydney.com
APN
APN
YOUNG AND JACKSON
HOTEL
EST
1875
YOUNG & JACKSON
The all new GLC
Hop On Hop Off
24
City SightSeeing
Melbourne
PT
59
TRG

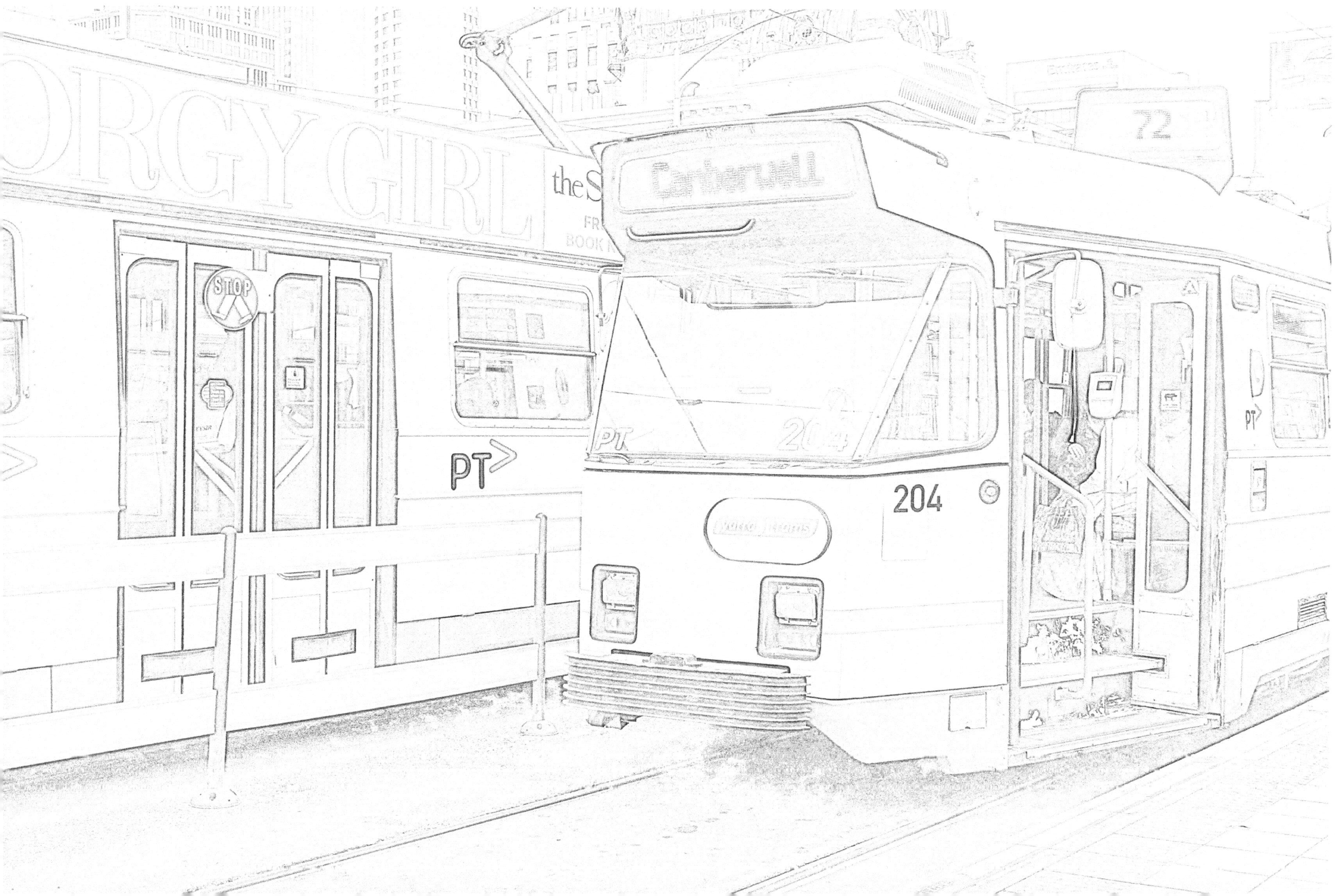
ORGY GIRL
the S
STOP
PT
Camberwell
72
204
PT
204

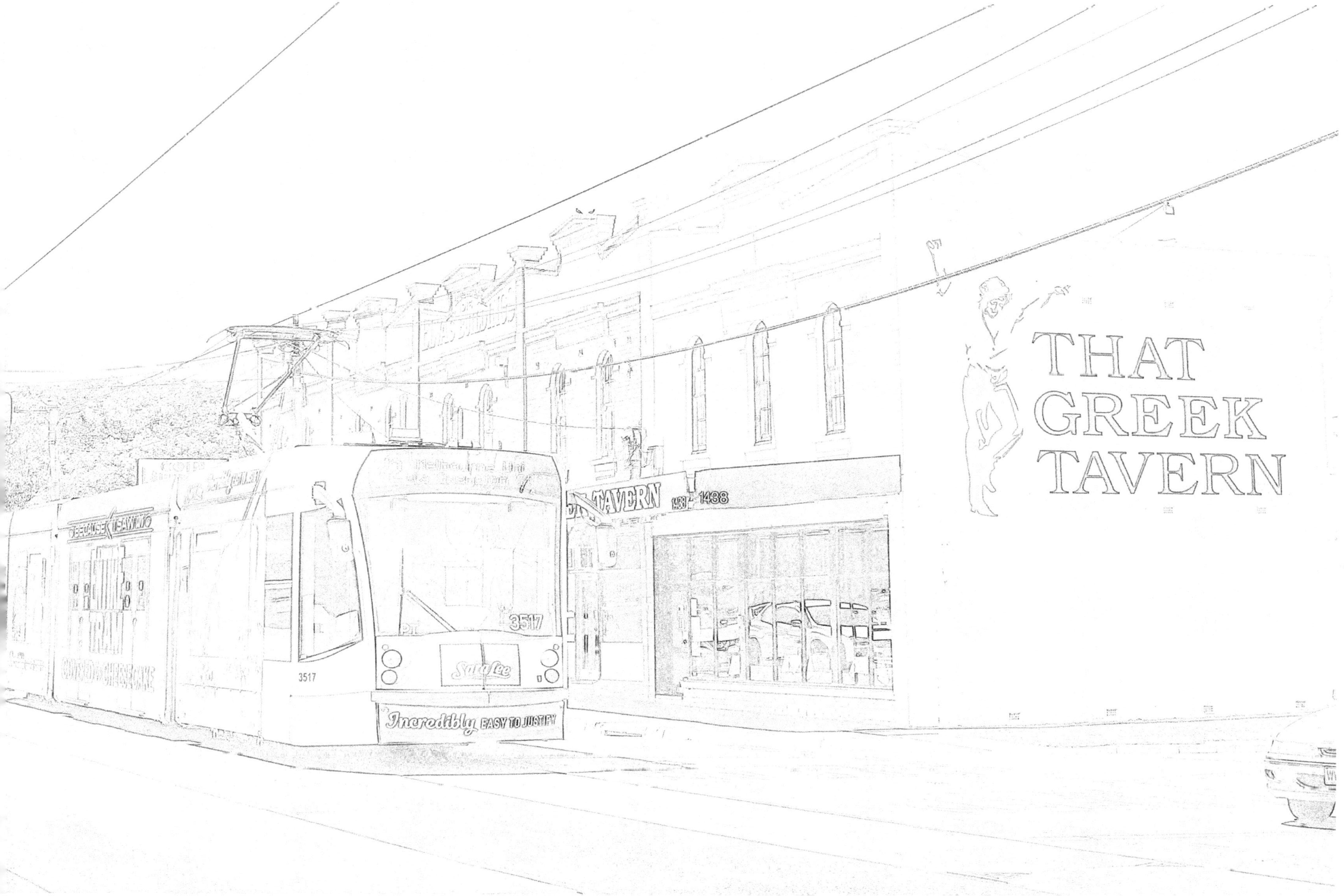
THAT
GREEK
TAVERN
TAVERN
1438
3517
Sara Lee
Incredibly EASY TO JUSTIFY
3517

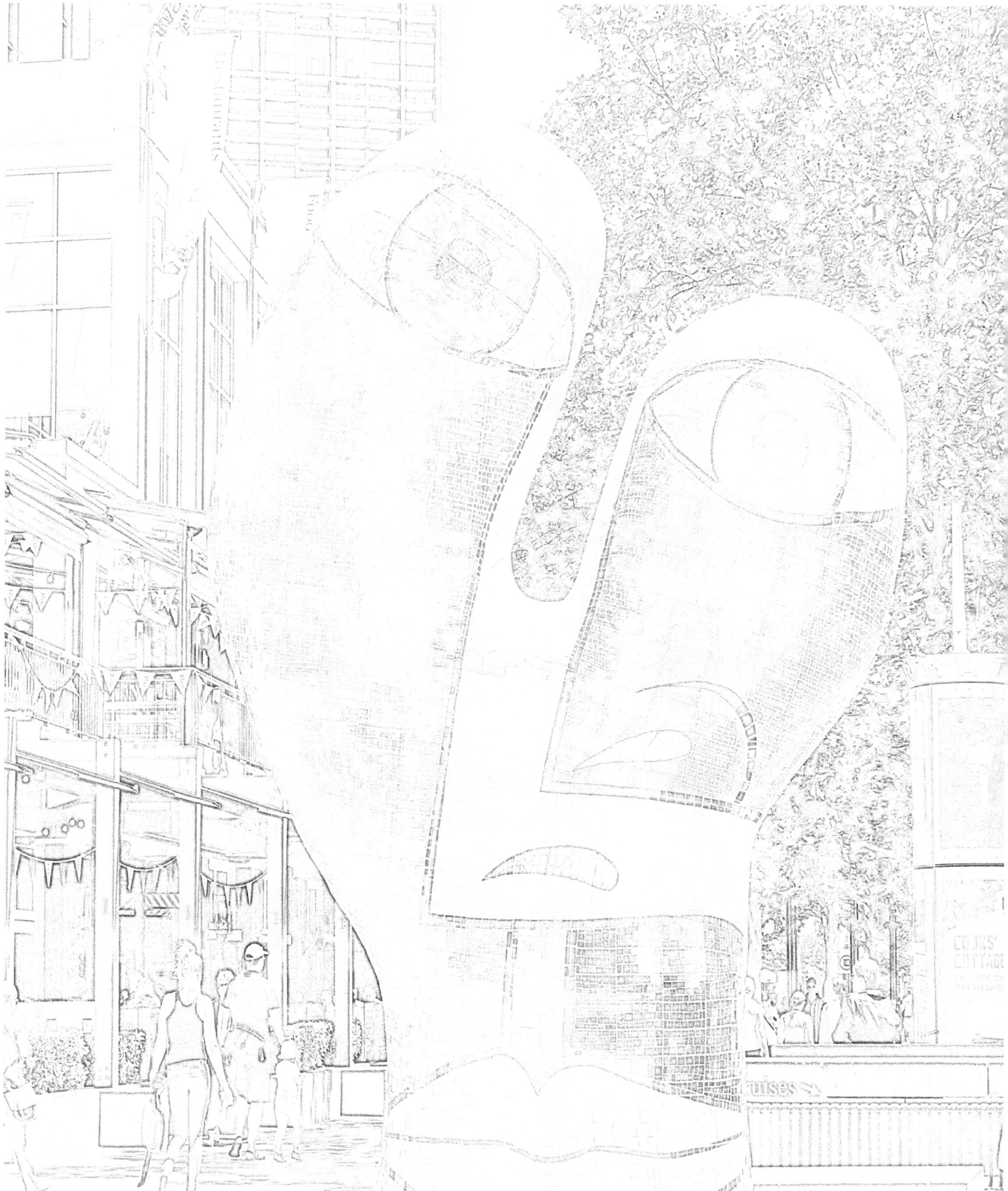

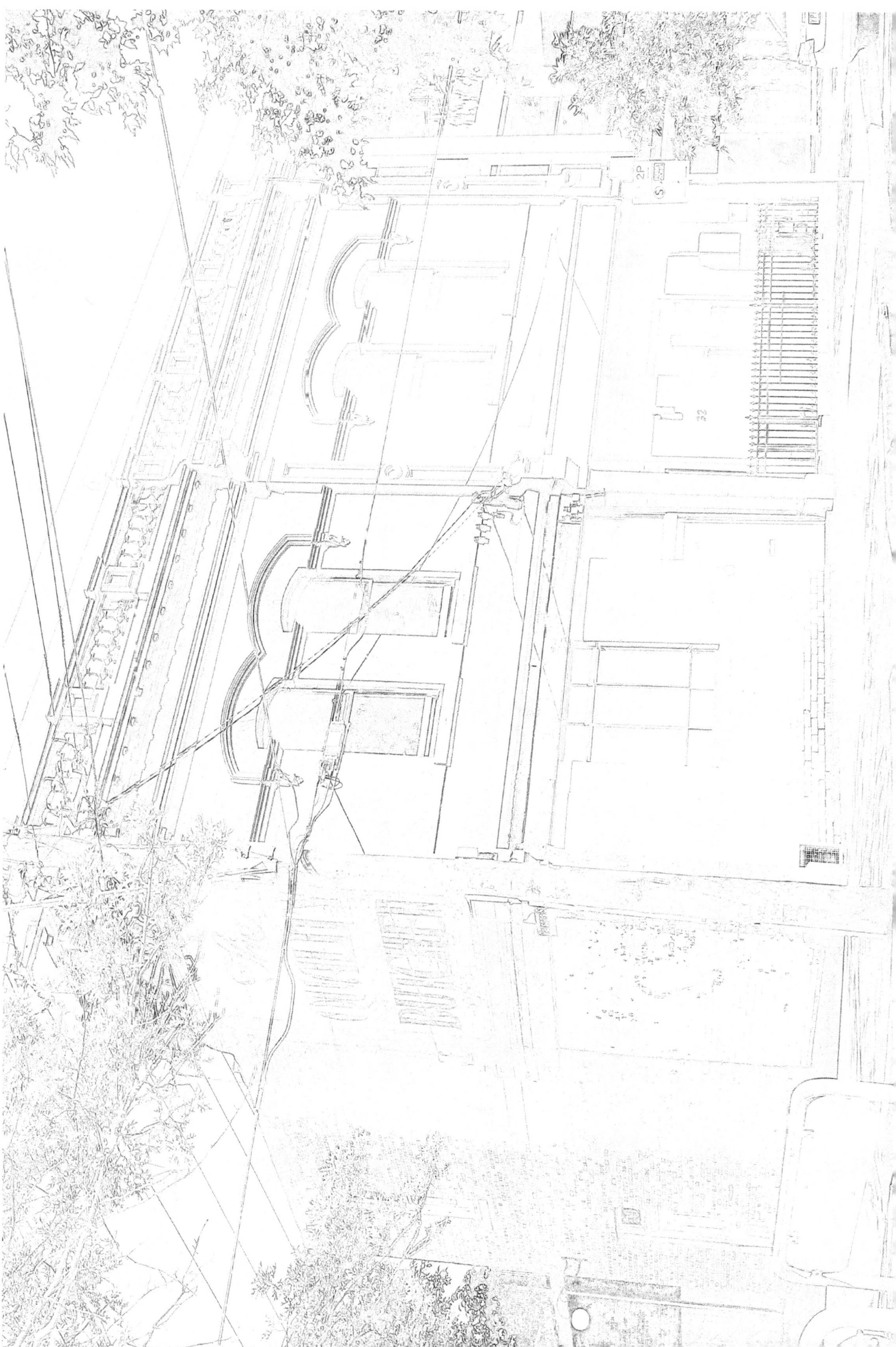
2P

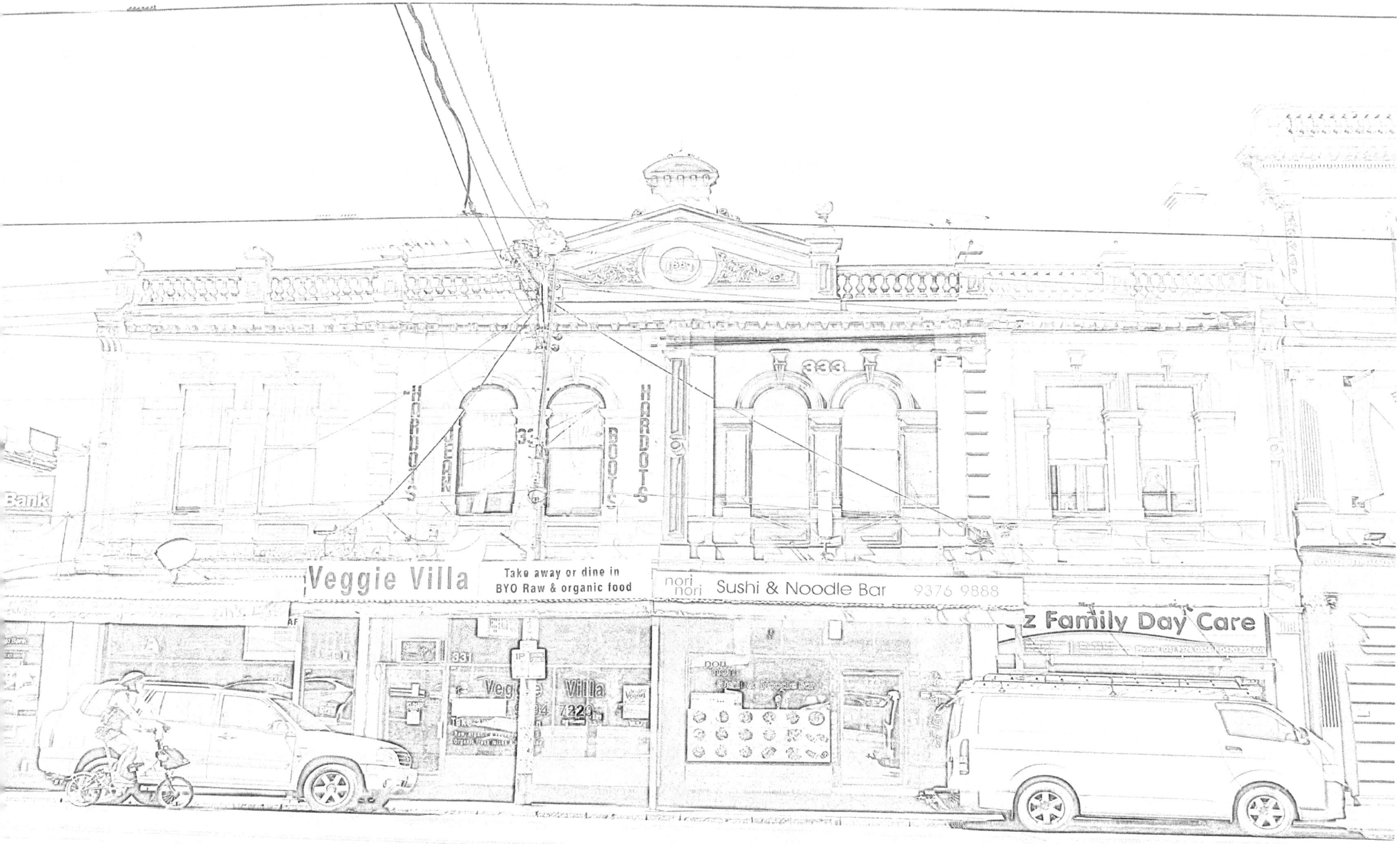

Veggie Villa
Take away or dine in
BYO Raw & organic food
nori nori
Sushi & Noodle Bar
9376 9888
333
331
Family Day Care
Bank

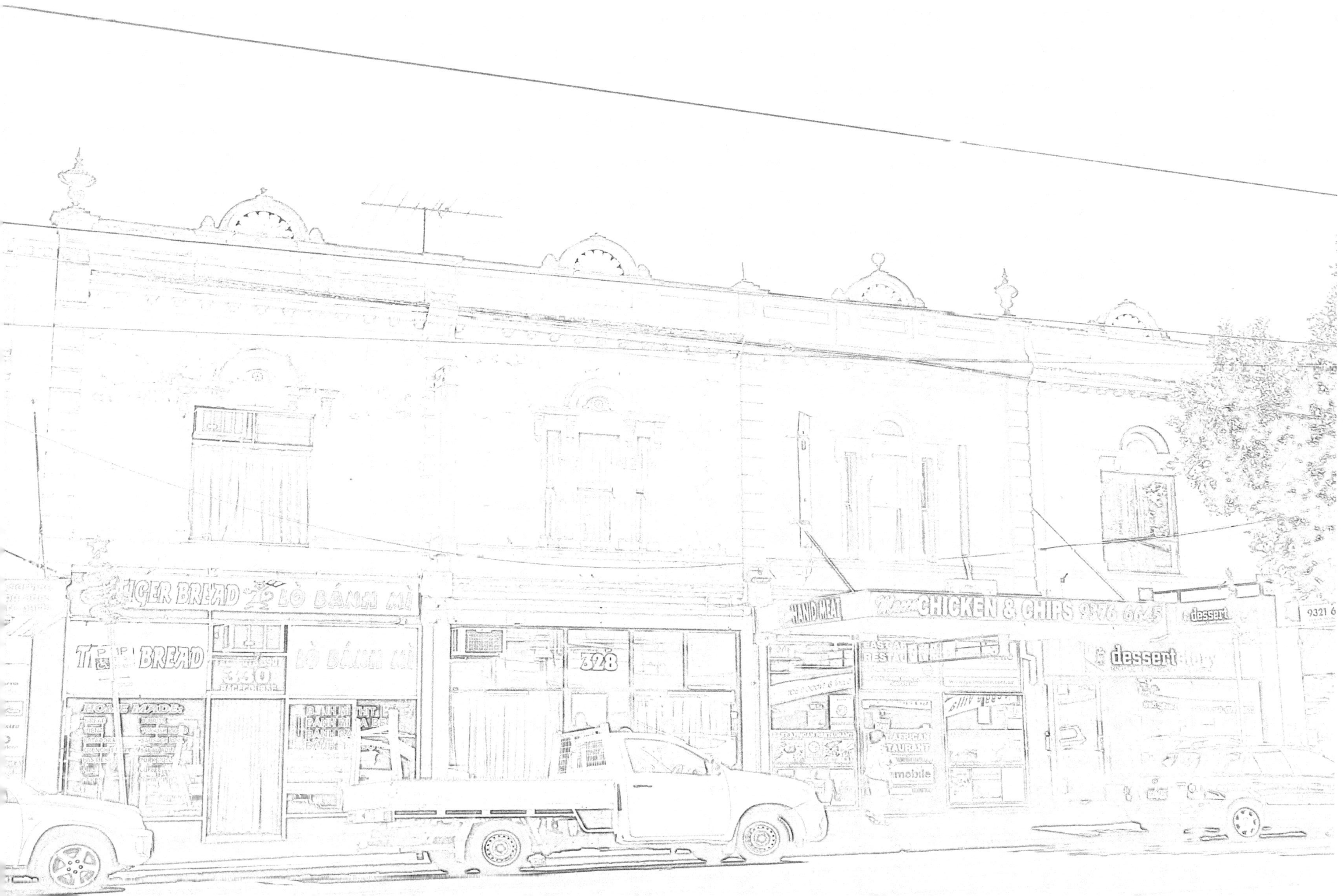

LÒ BÁNH MÌ
CHICKEN & CHIPS 9376 6645
dessert
328
dessert

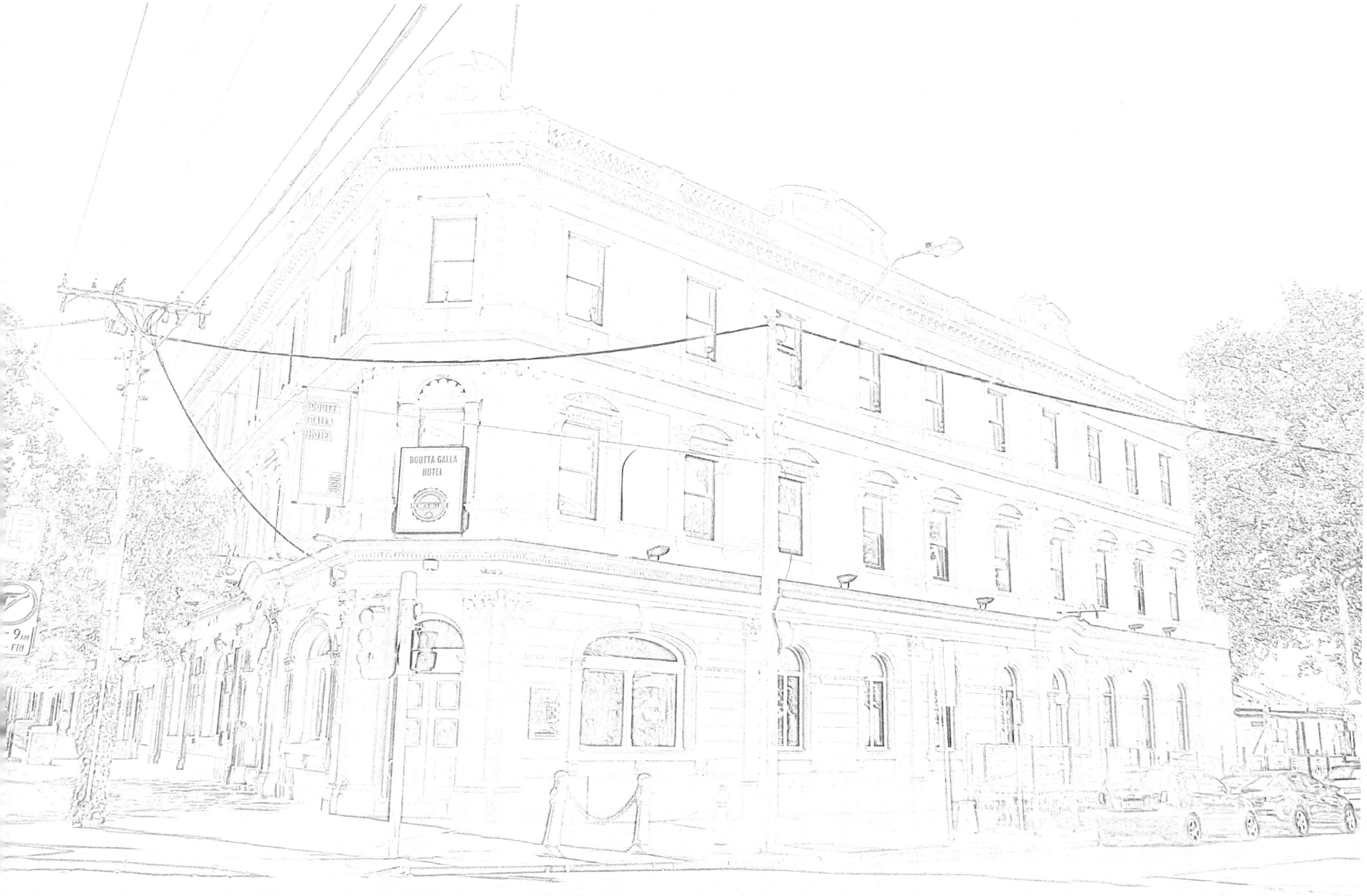
DOUTTA GALLA HOTEL
DOUTTA GALLA HOTEL
9AM
FRI

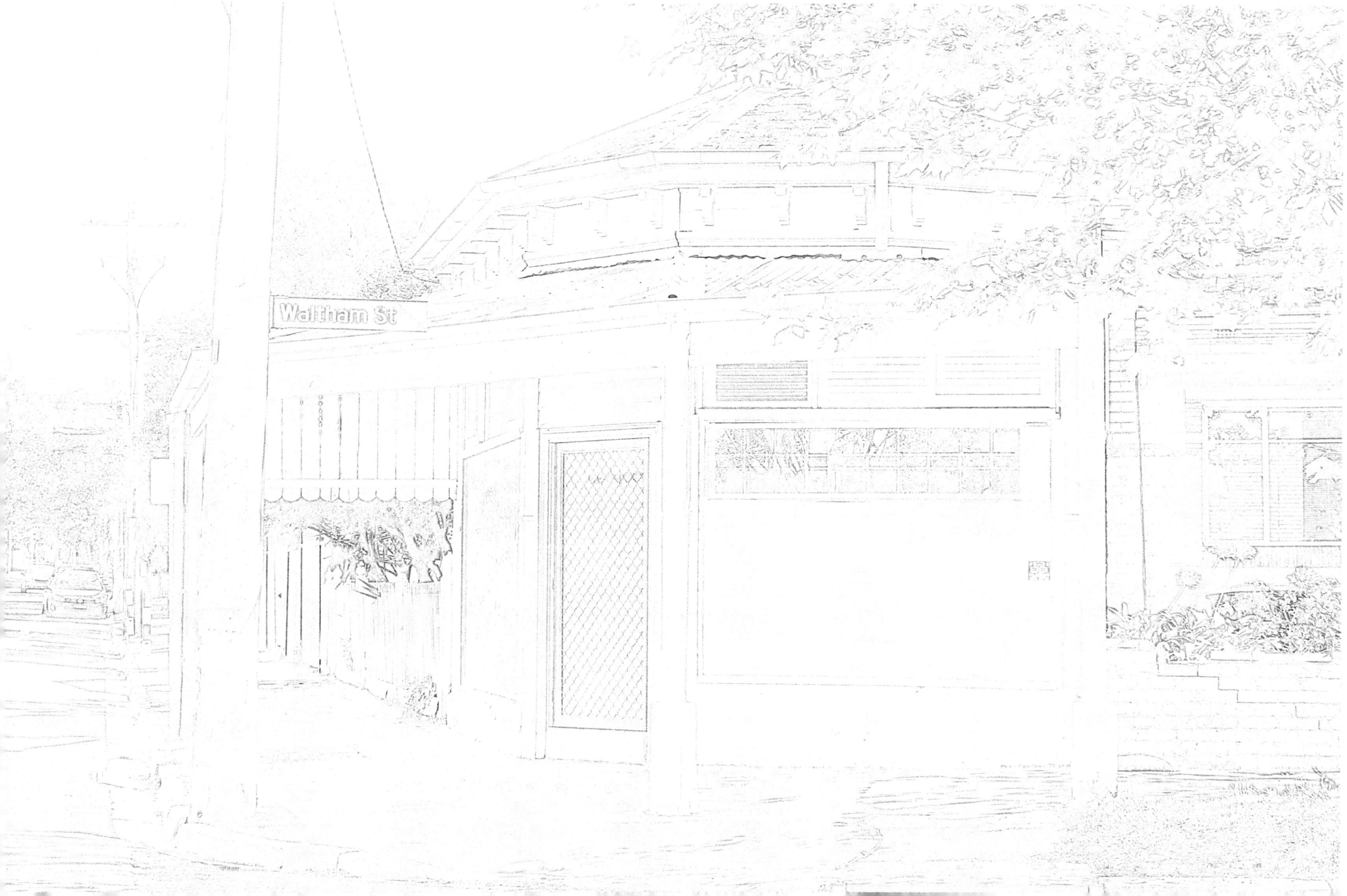
Waltham St

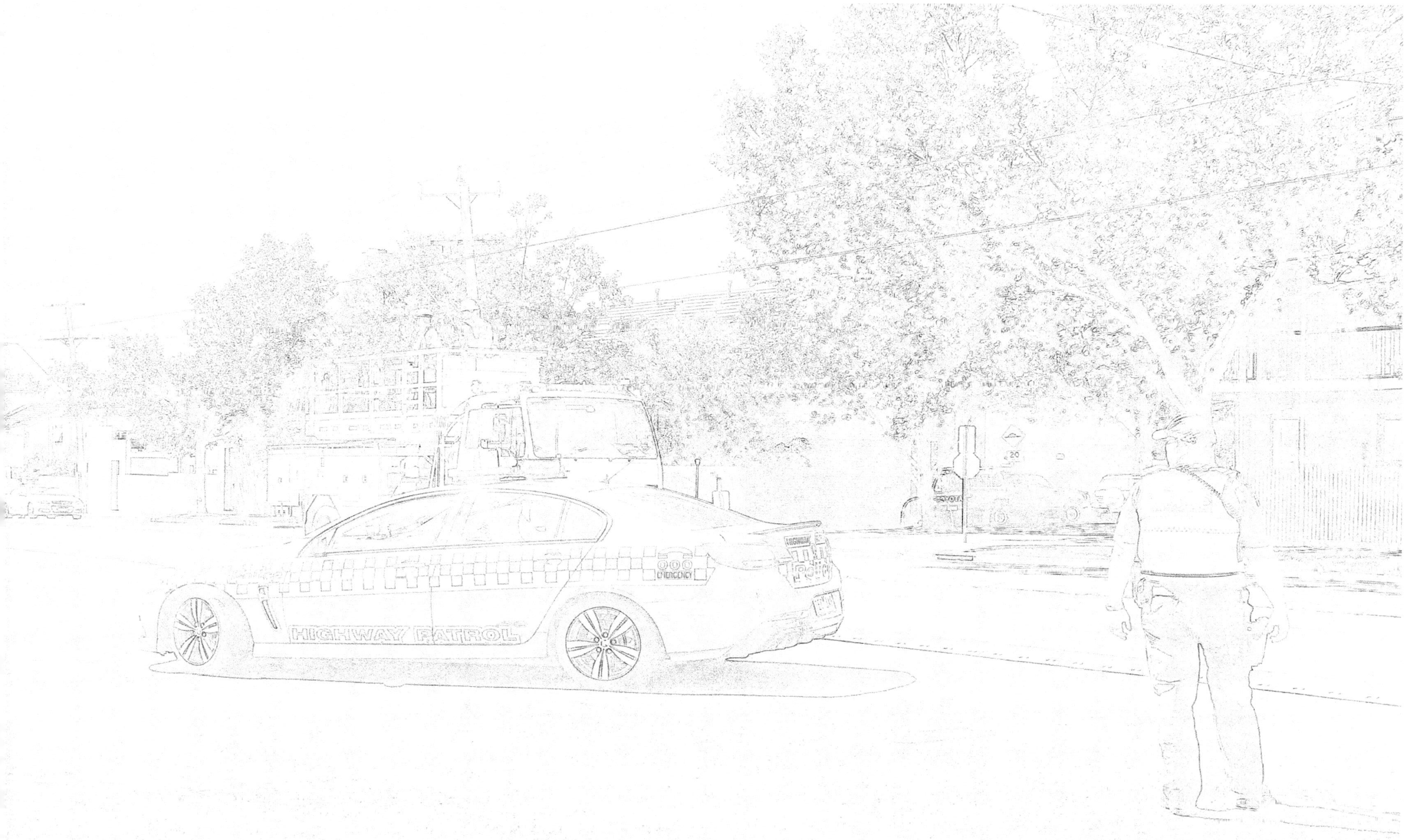
HIGHWAY PATROL
000
EMERGENCY
POLICE

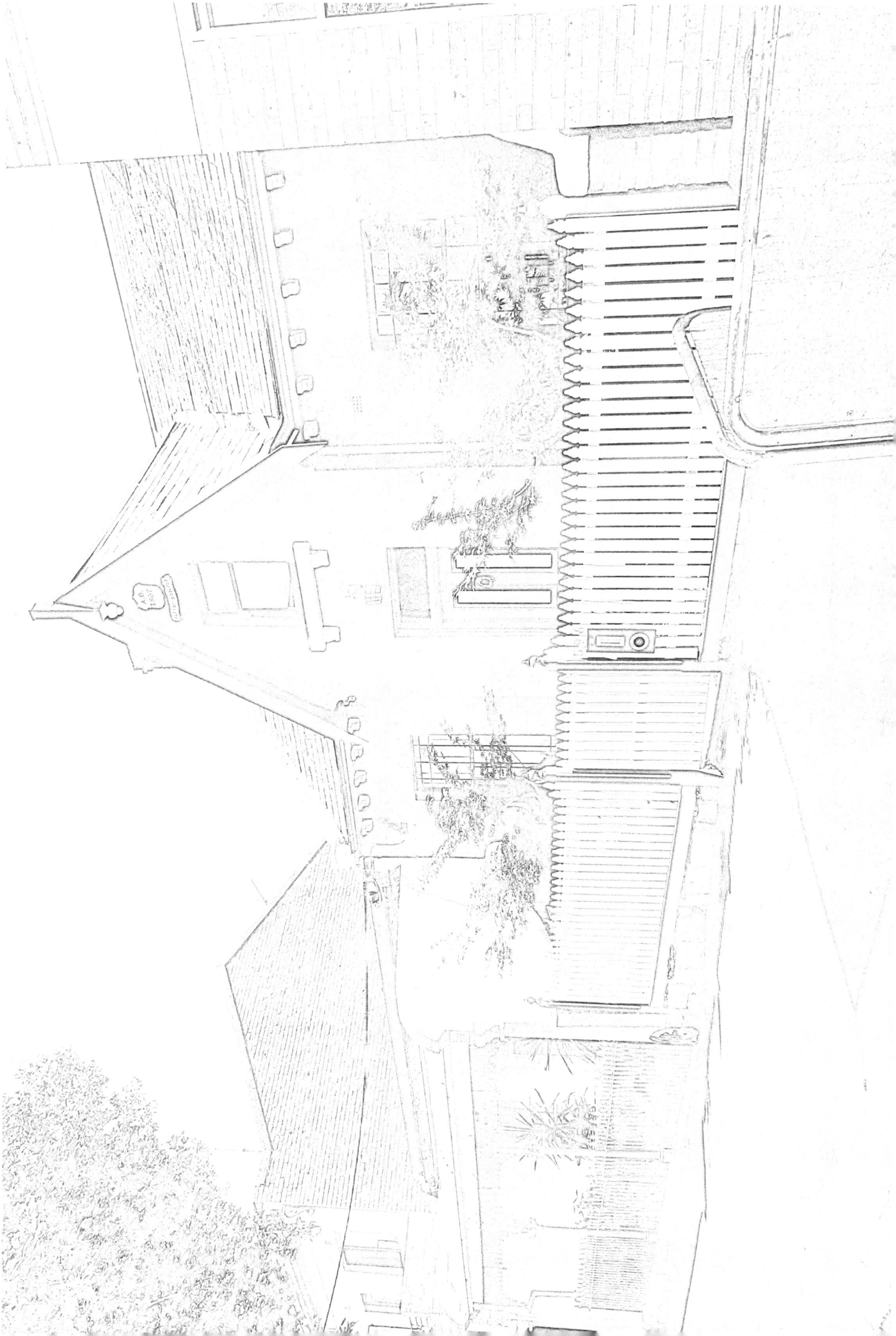

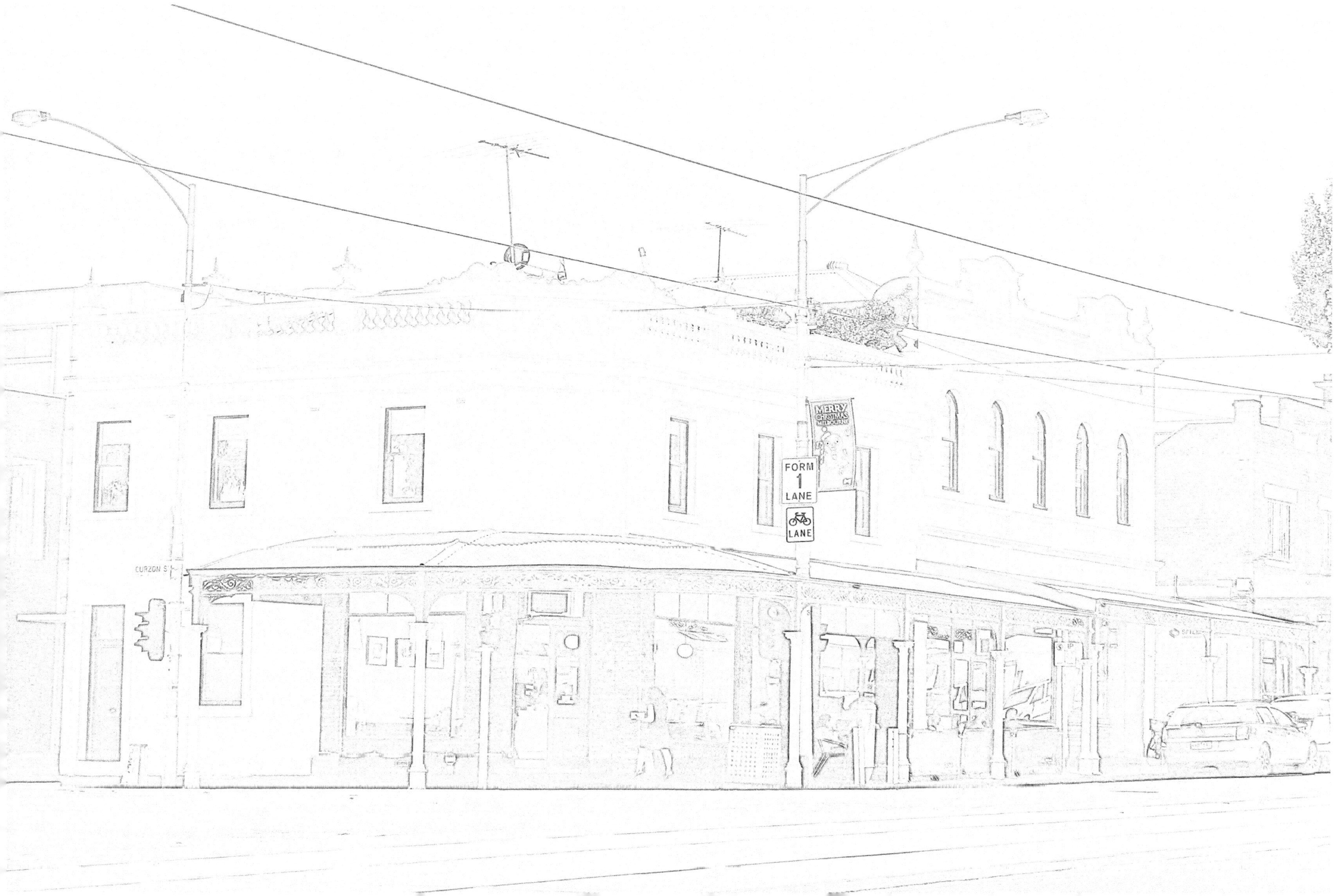
MERRY CHRISTMAS
FORM 1 LANE
LANE

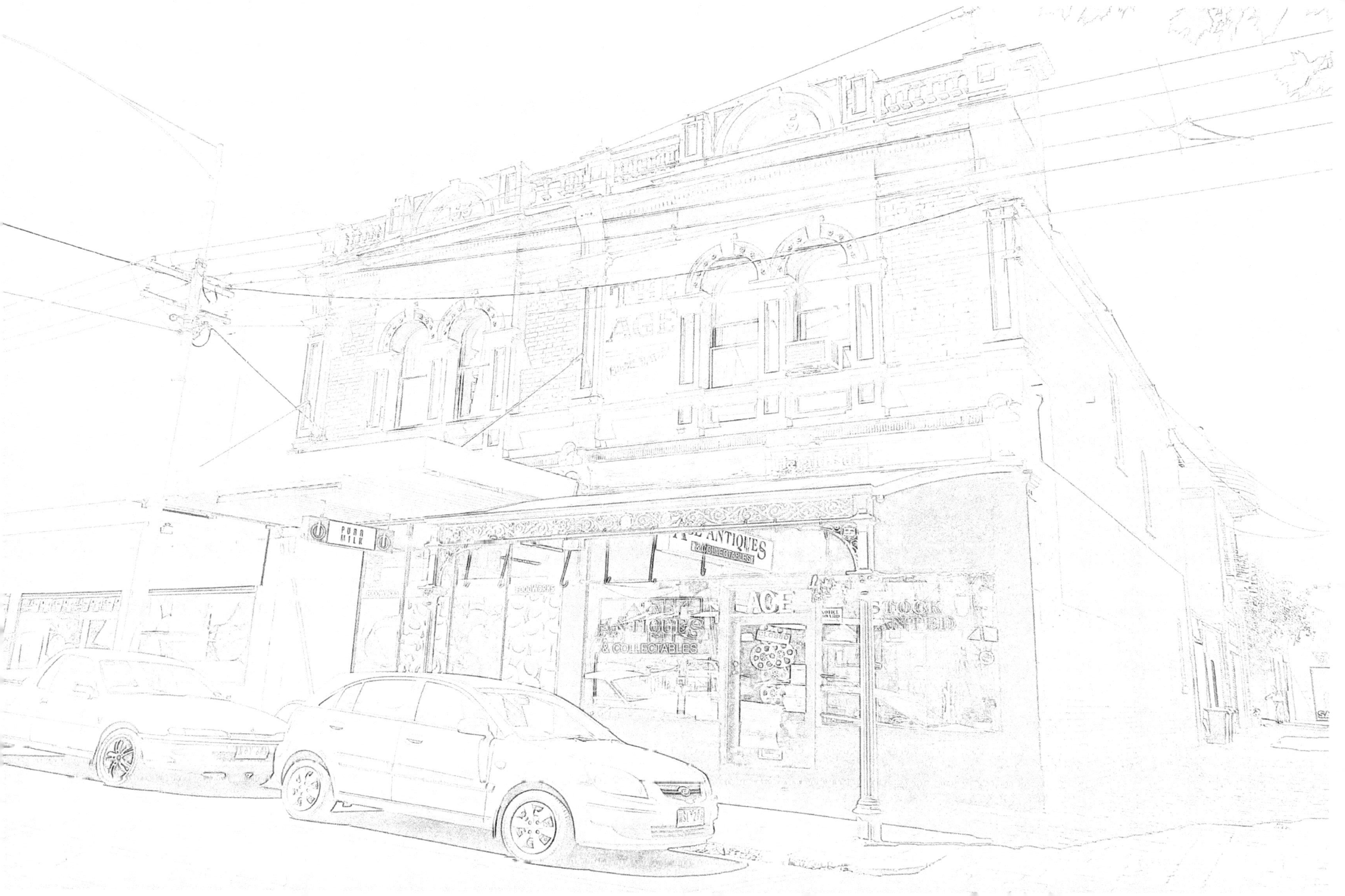
PURA MILK
ANTIQUES
& COLLECTABLES
ACE
ANTIQUES
& COLLECTABLES
STOCK
FOODWORKS

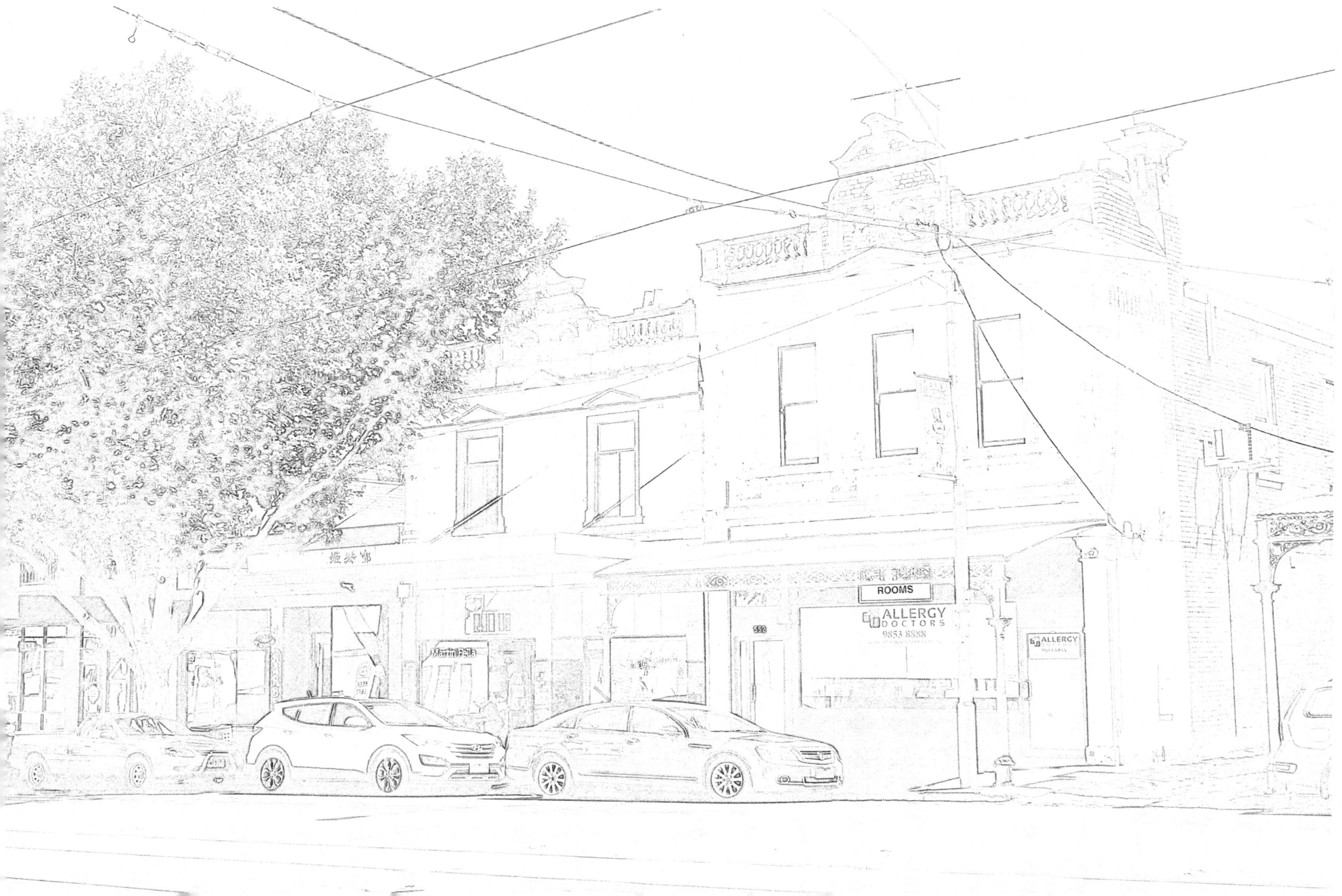
ROOMS
ALLERGY
DOCTORS
9853 8888
552
ALLERGY
Martin Pella

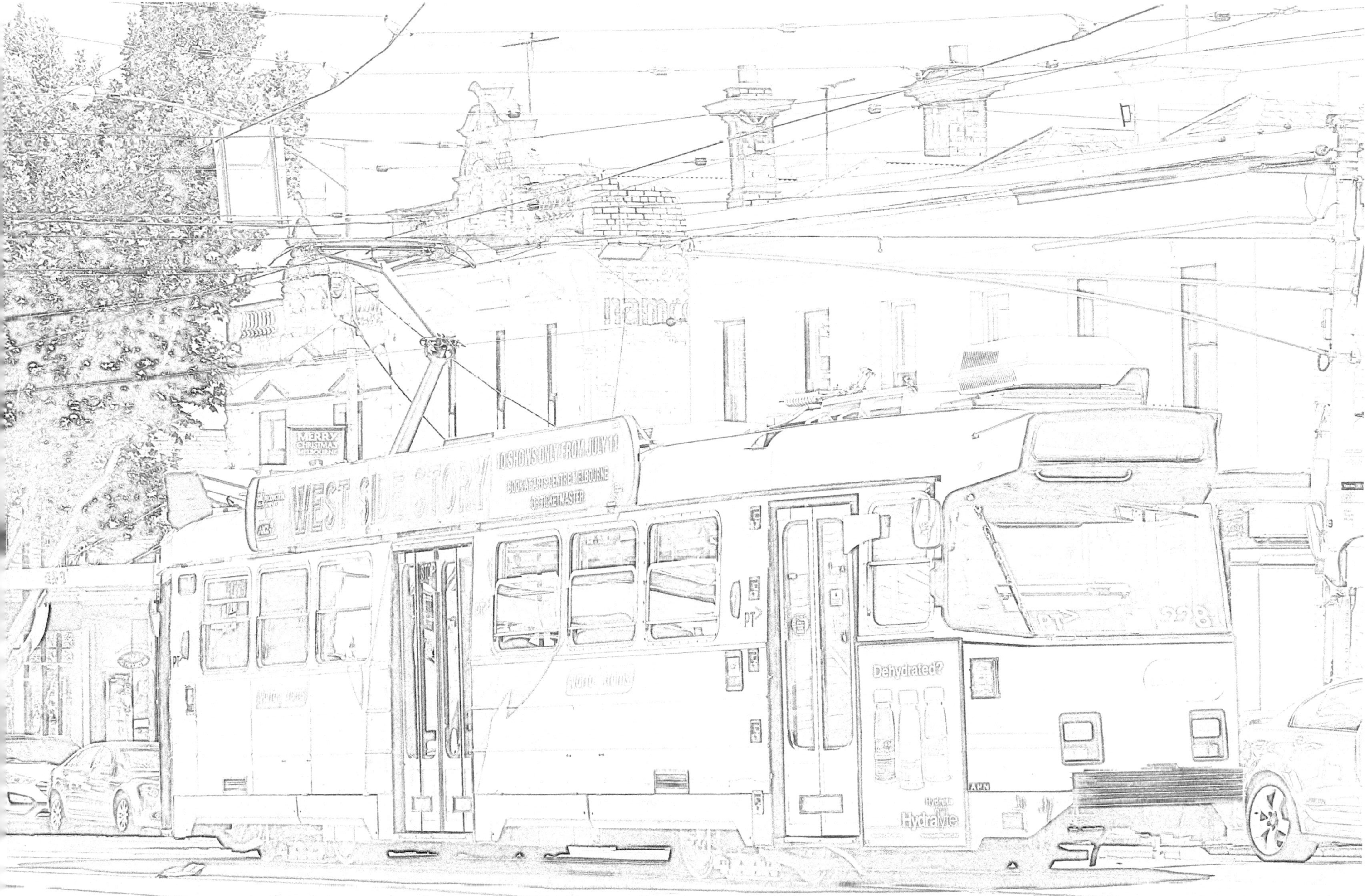
WEST SIDE STORY
10 SHOWS ONLY FROM JULY 11
BOOK AT ARTS CENTRE MELBOURNE
OR TICKETMASTER
MERRY
CHRISTMAS
MELBOURNE
Dehydrated?
Hydralyte
228

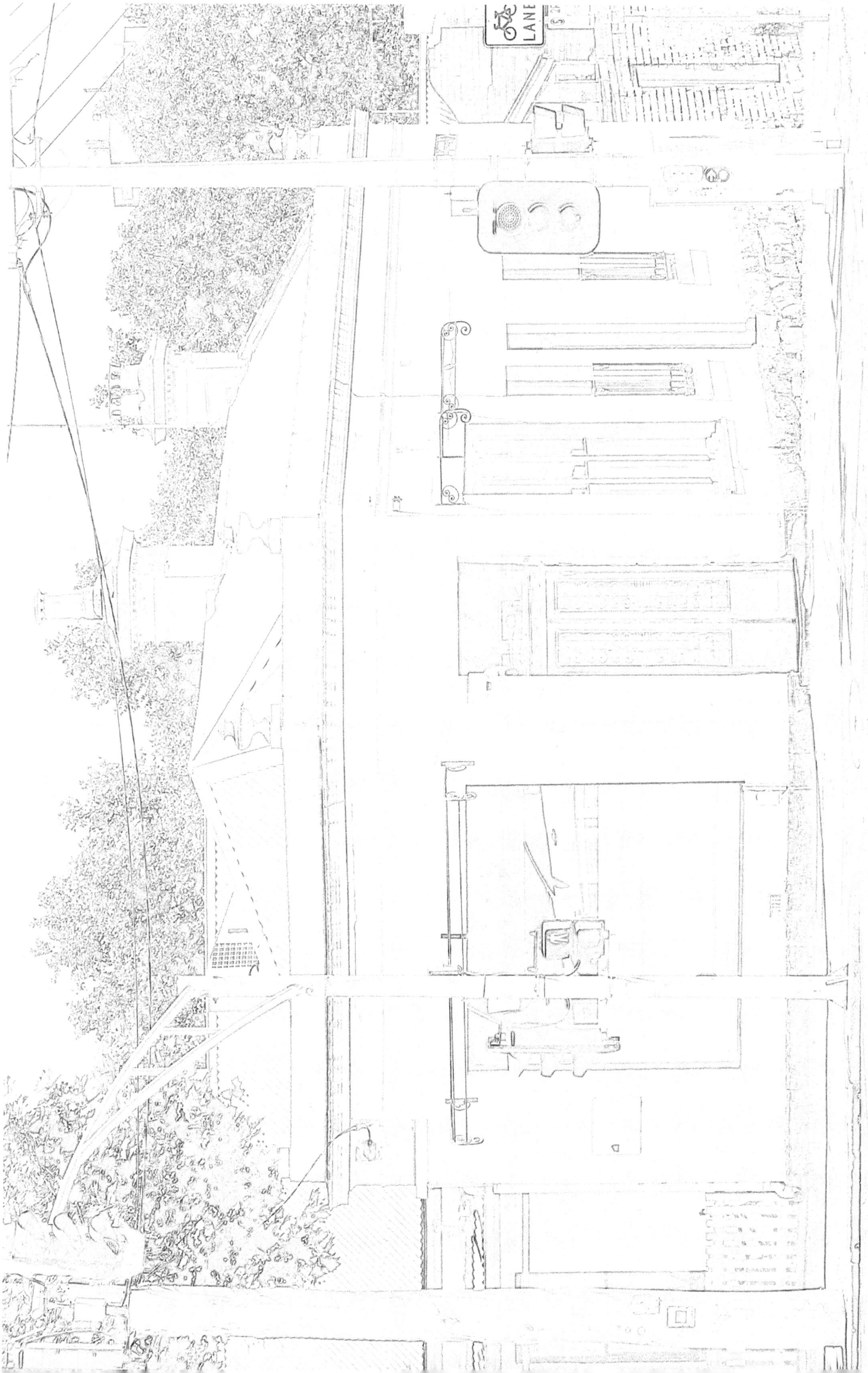
LANE

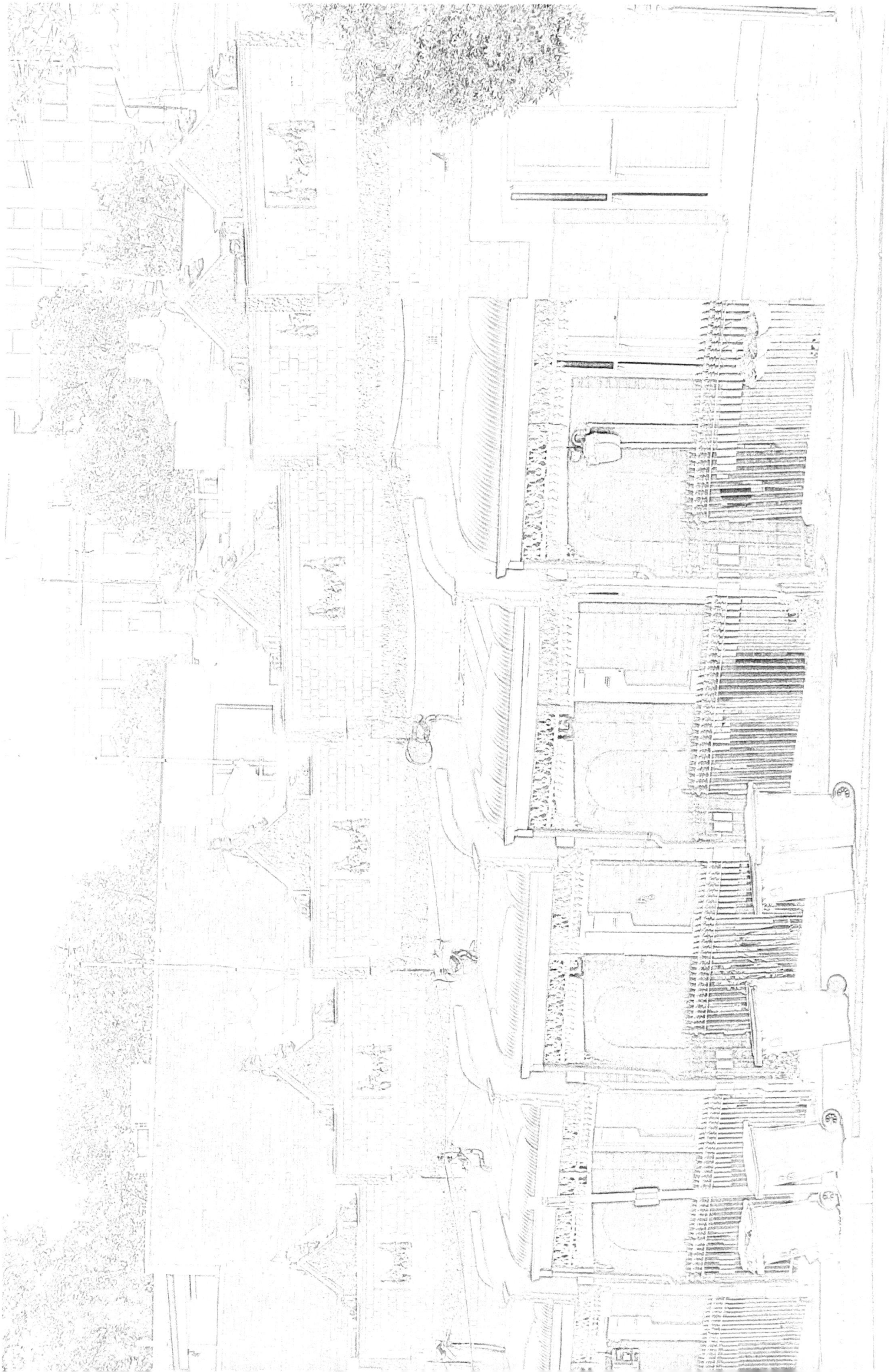

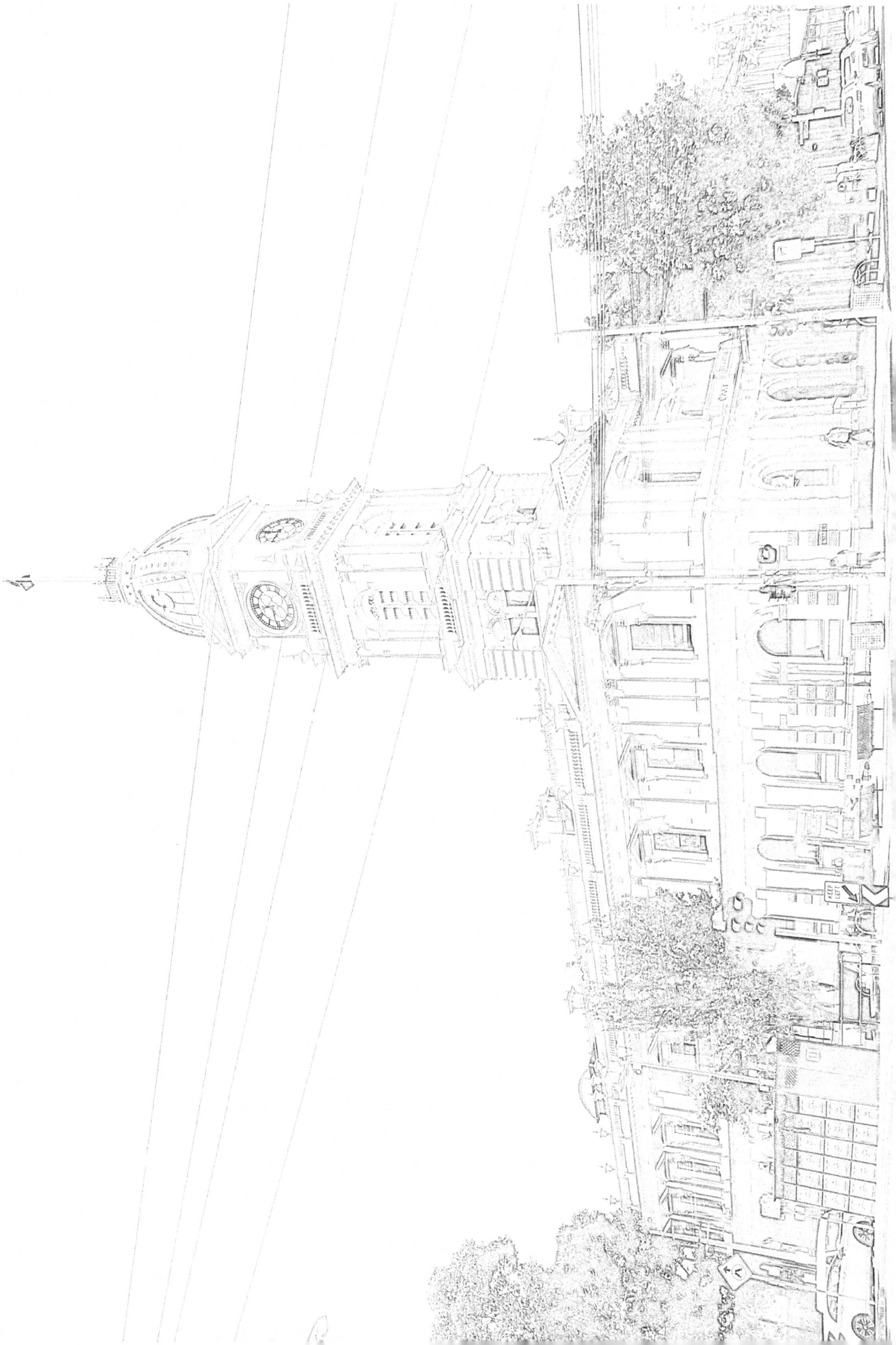

POSTshop

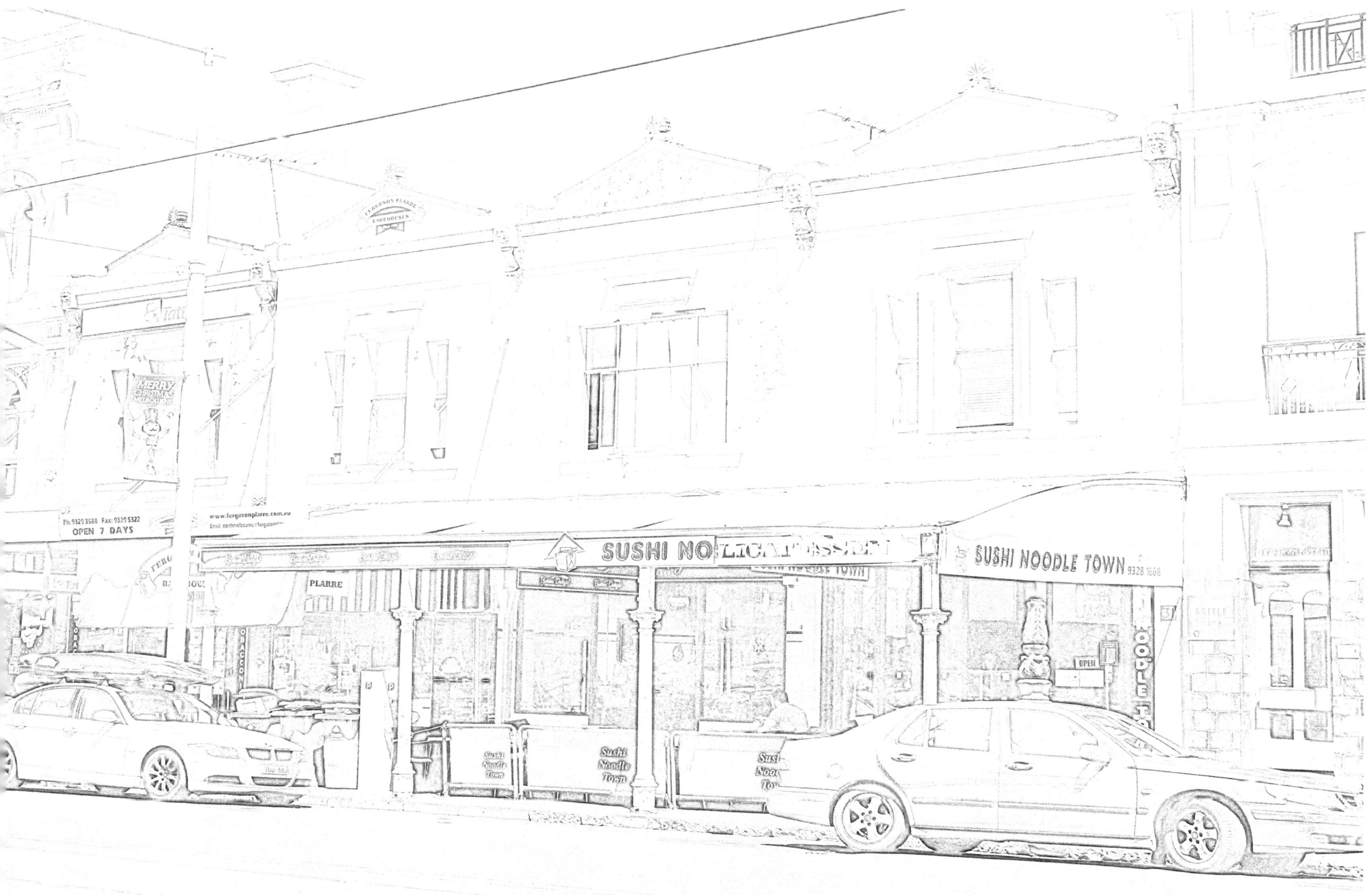
SUSHI NOODLE TOWN 9328 1668
SUSHI NO
PLARRE
OPEN 7 DAYS
www.fergusonplarre.com.au
MERRY CHRISTMAS
OPEN
Sushi Noodle Town
Sushi Noodle Town

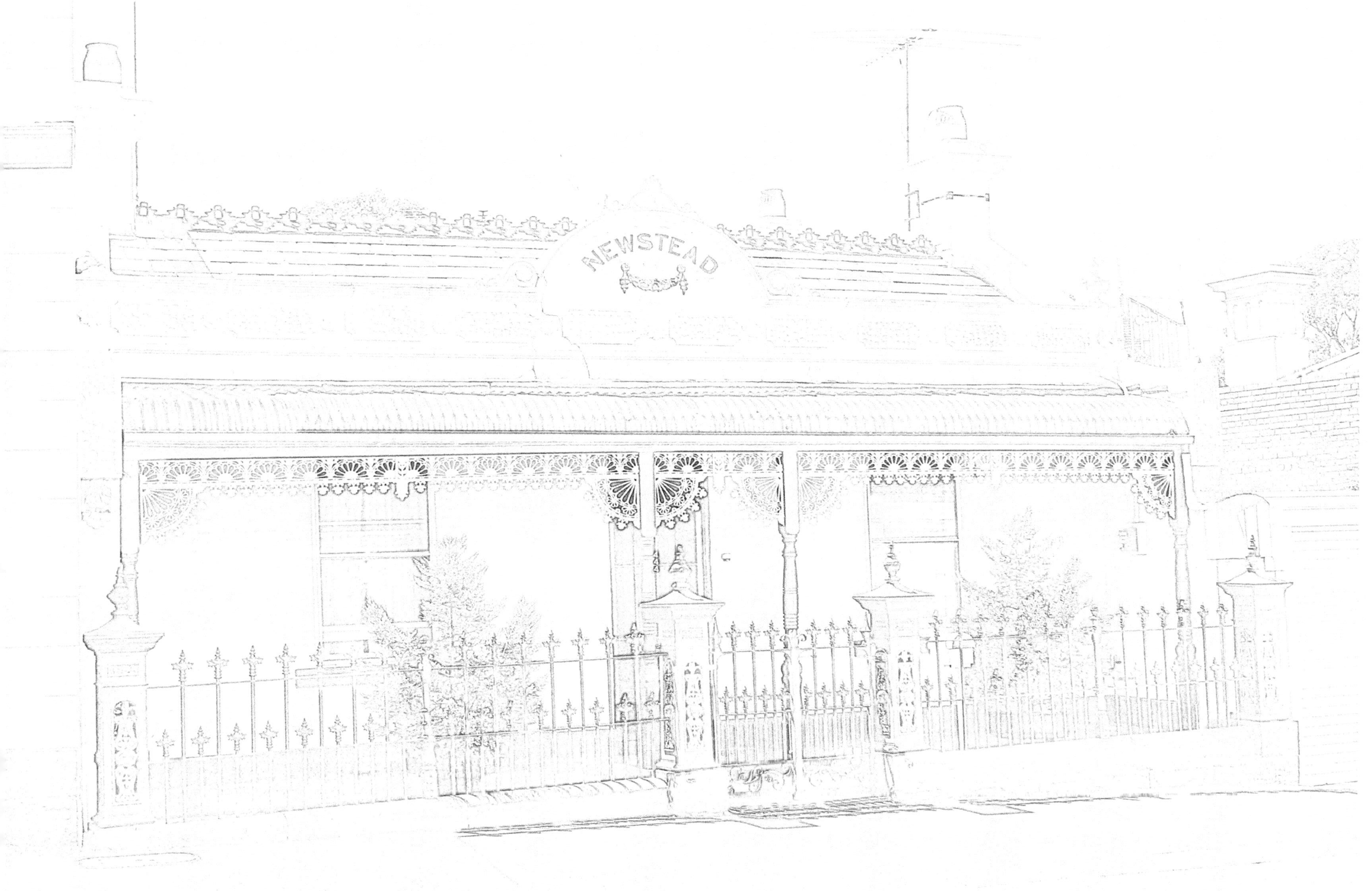
NEWSTEAD

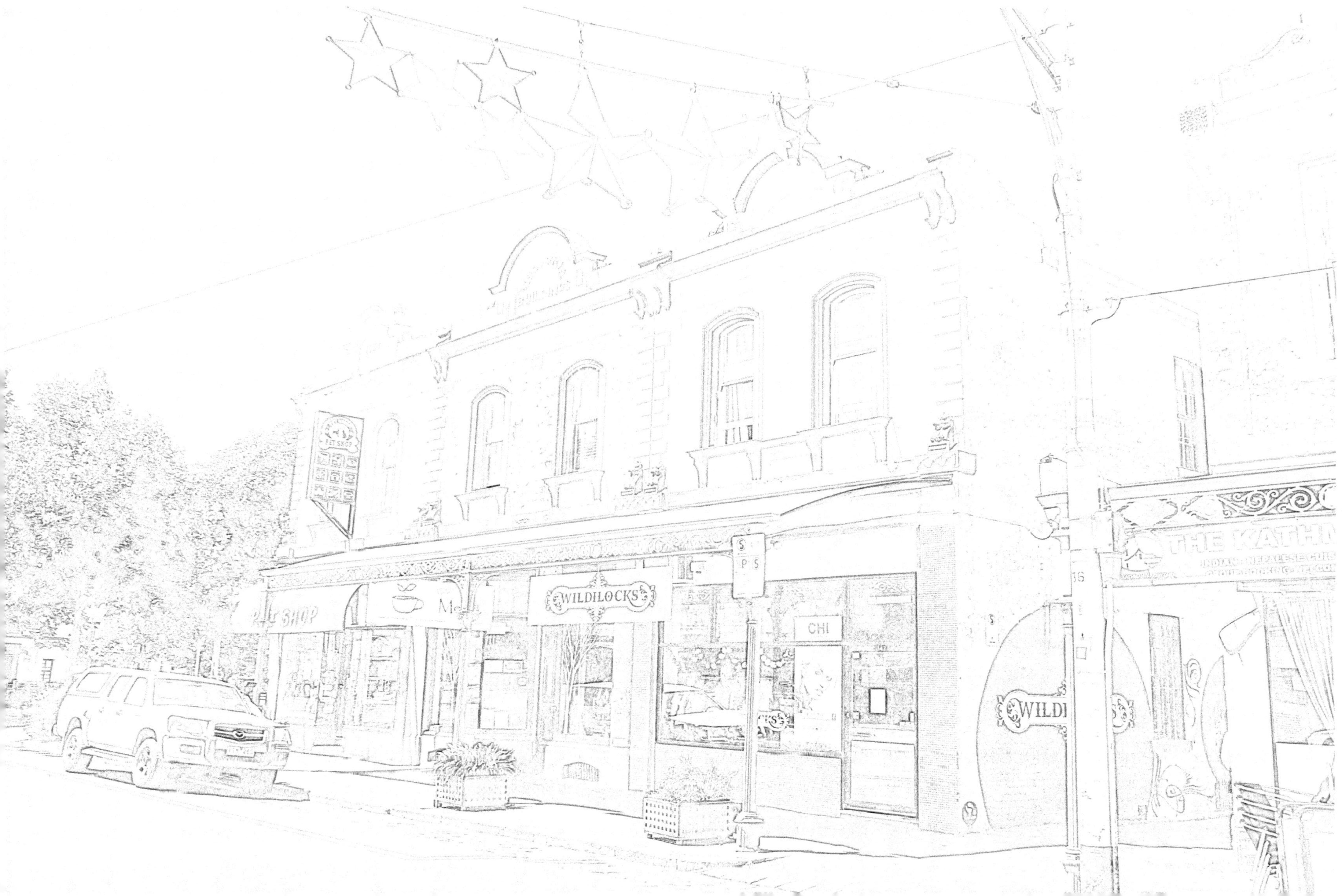
WILDILOCKS
CHI
THE KATHM
S
P S
36

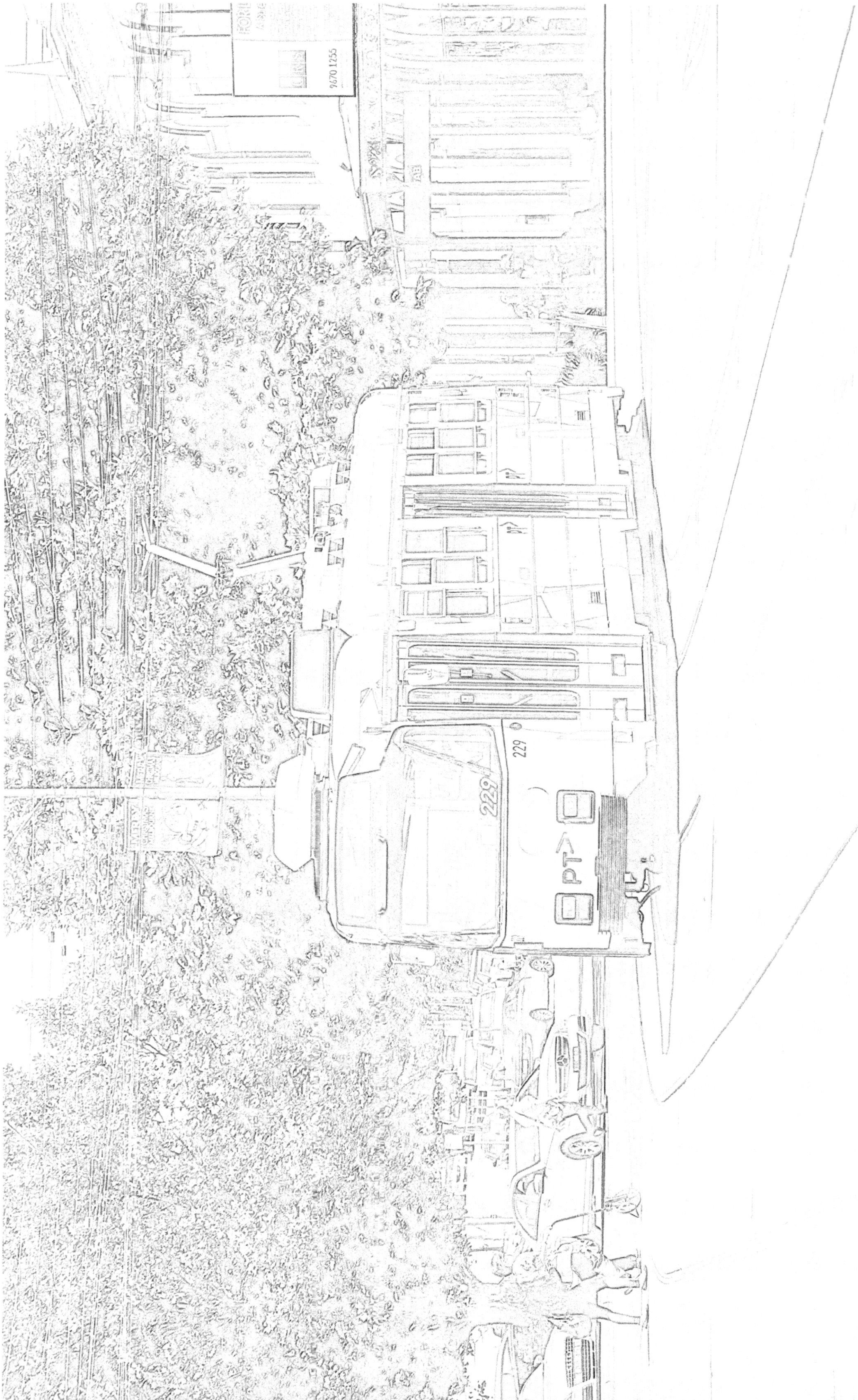
229
PT

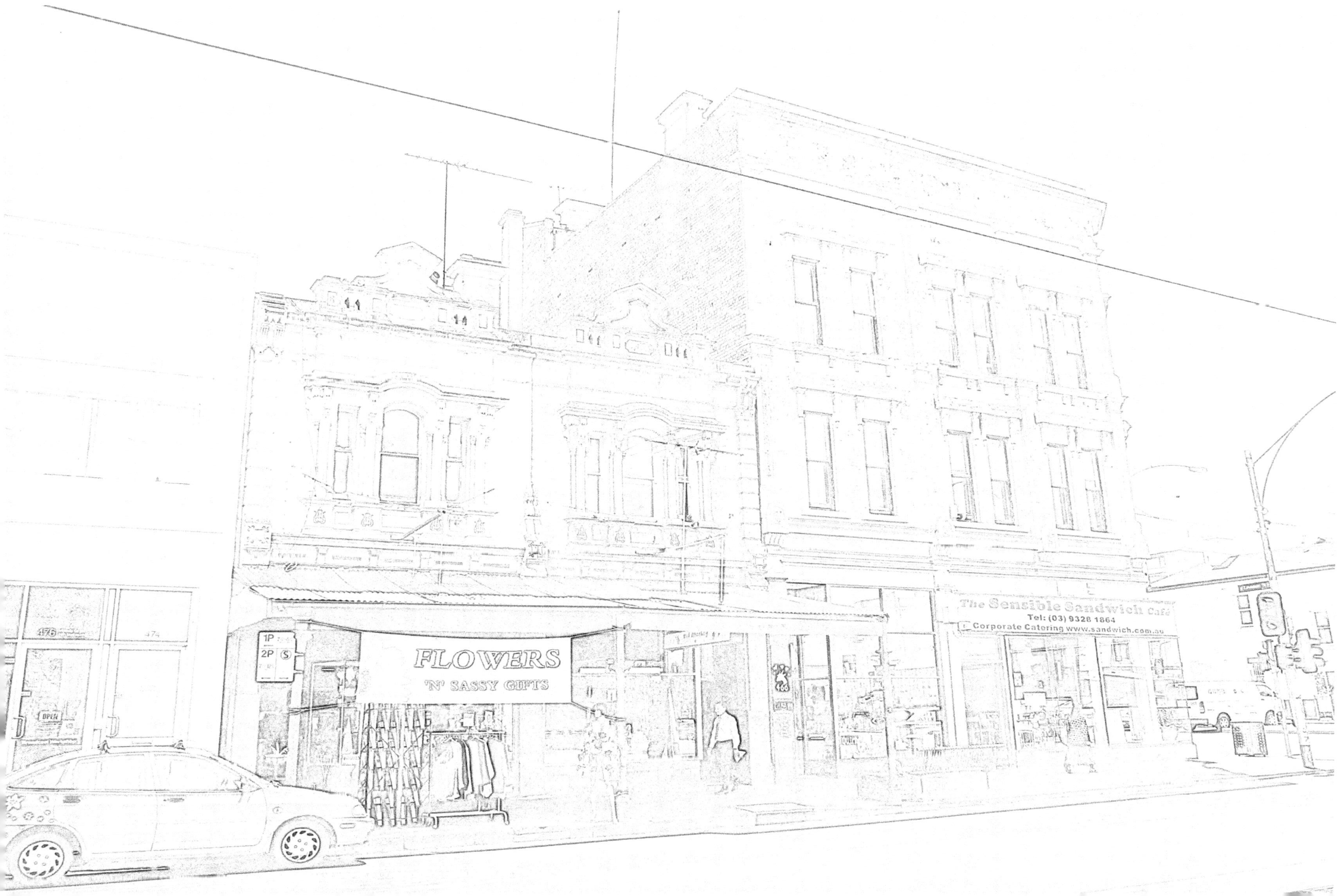
476
474
OPEN
1P
2P
FLOWERS
'N' SASSY GIFTS
The Sensible Sandwich Cafe
Tel: (03) 9328 1864
Corporate Catering www.sandwich.com.au

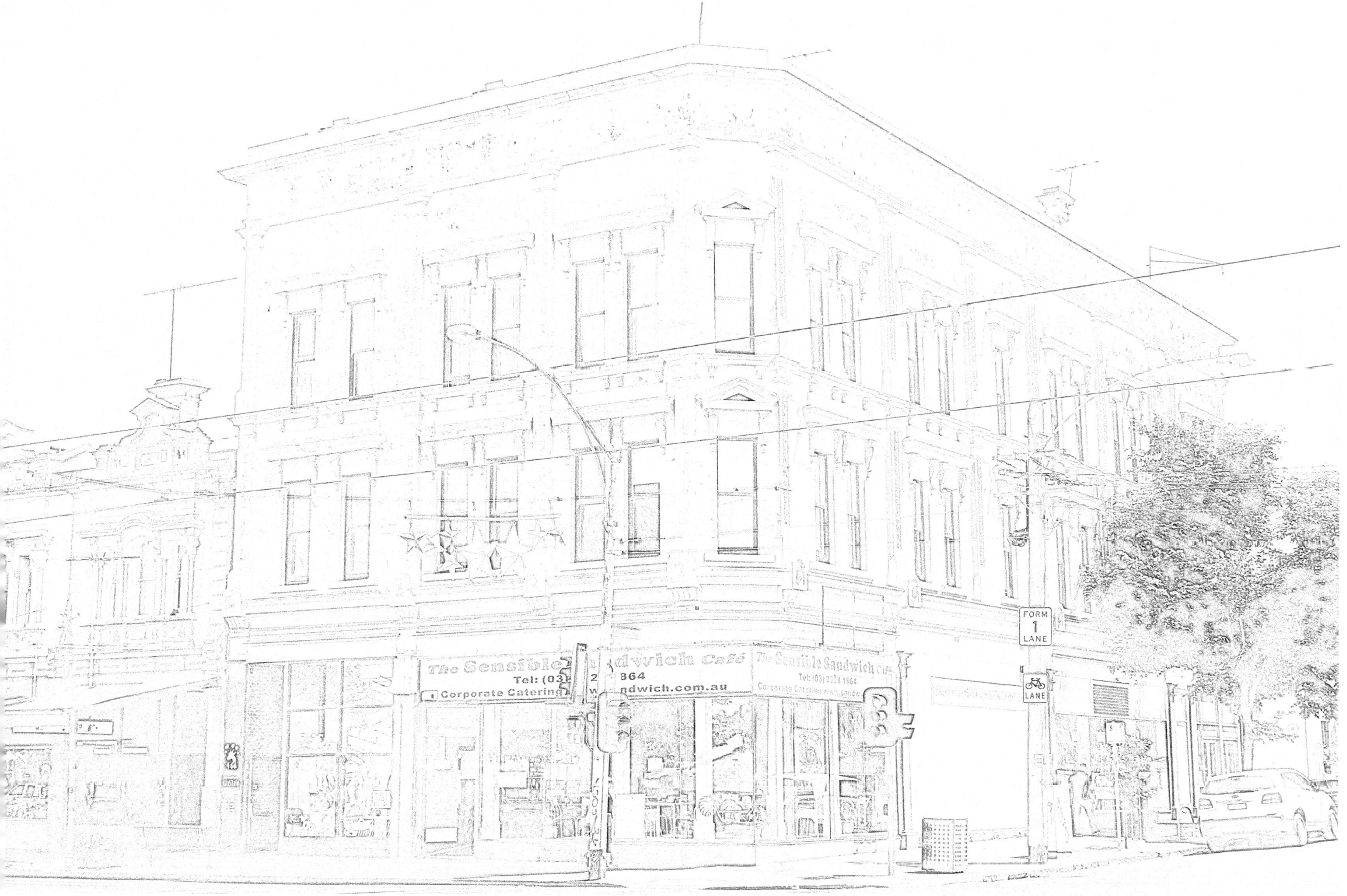
The Sensible Sandwich Café
Corporate Catering
The Sensible Sandwich Café
Tel: (03) 9328 1864
FORM
1
LANE
LANE

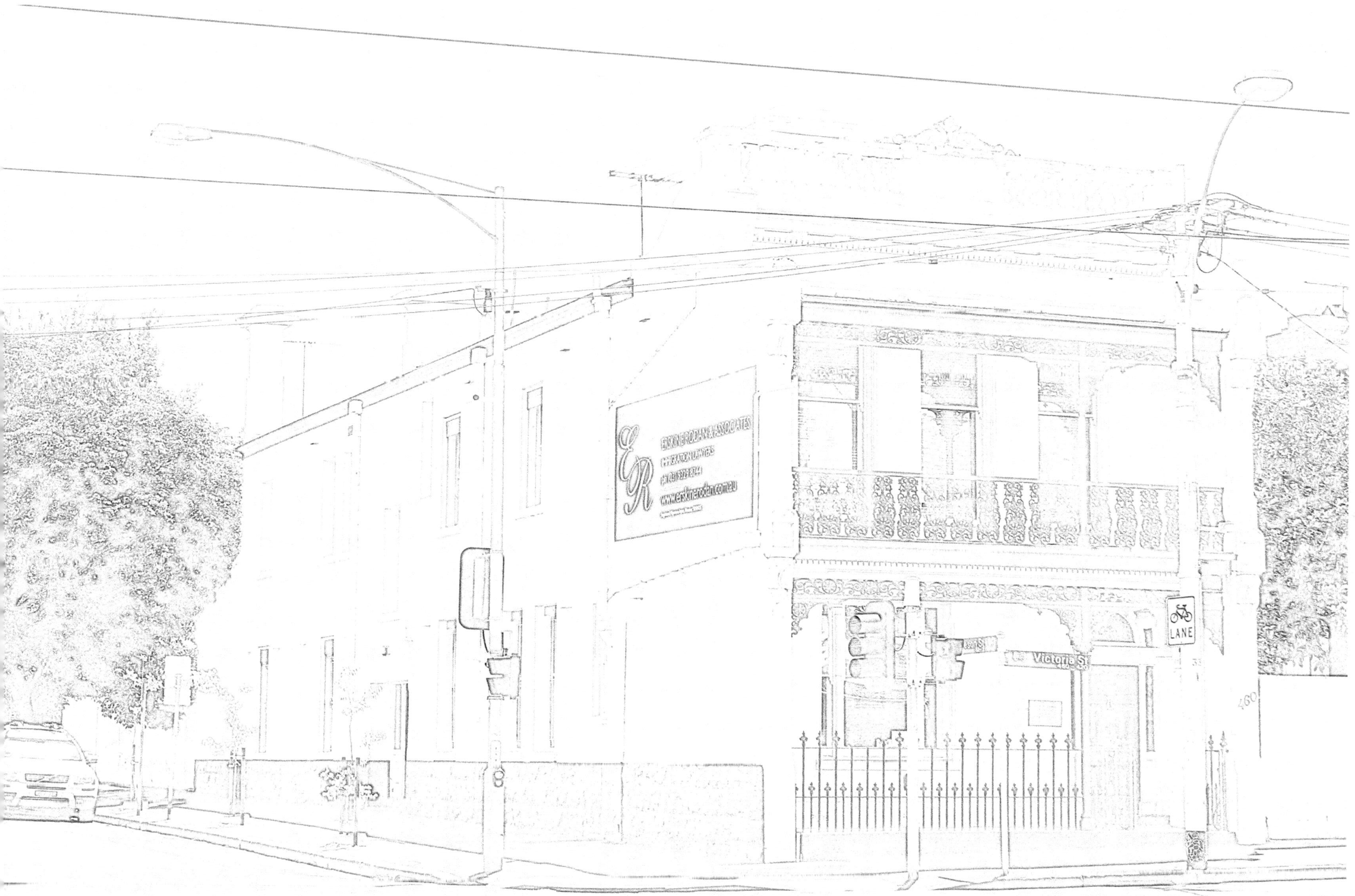
ERSKINE RODAN & ASSOCIATES
www.erskinerodan.com.au
LANE
Victoria St

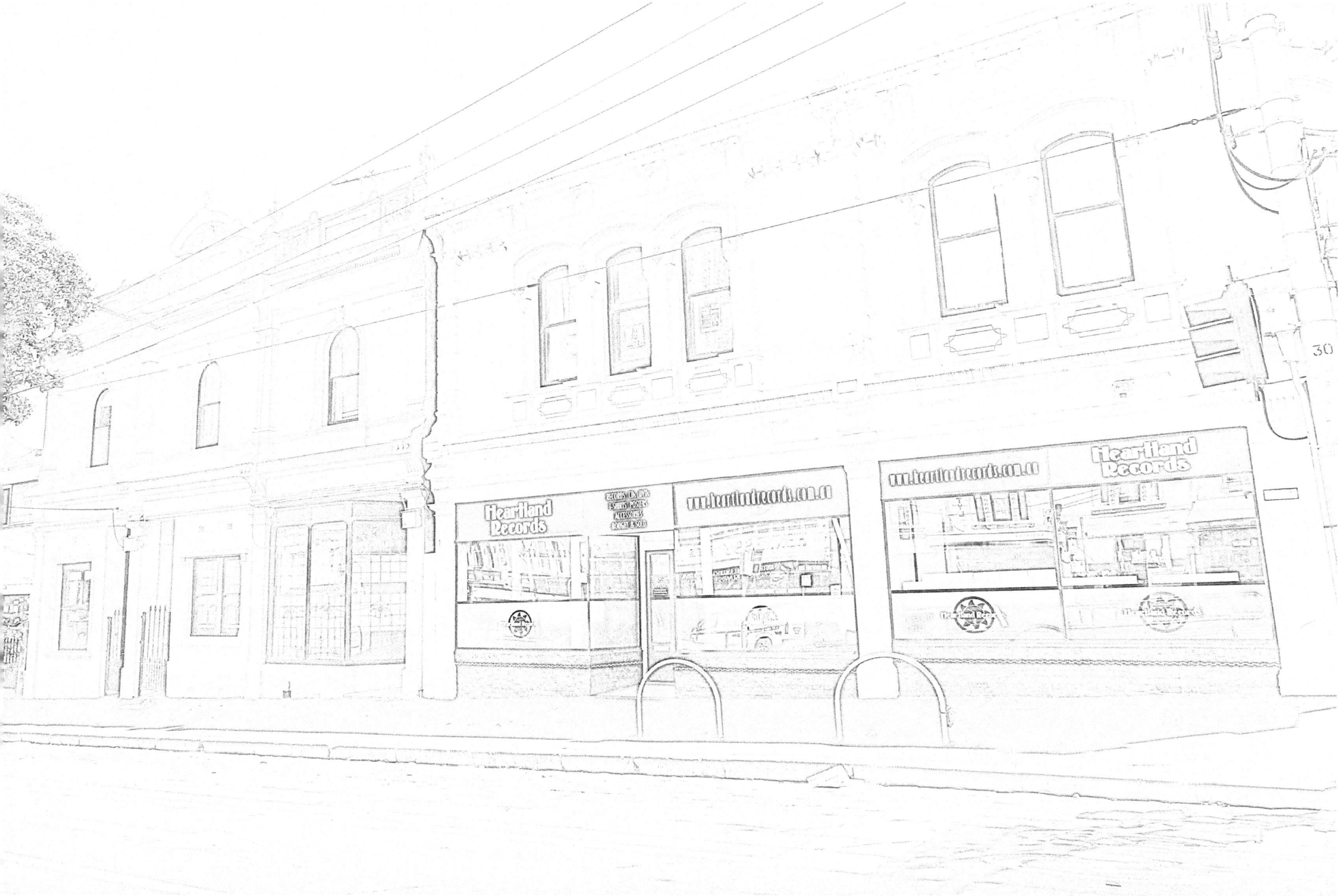
HeartLand Records
Records CDs DVDs
T-Shirts Posters
Accessories
Bought & Sold
www.heartlandrecords.com.au
www.heartlandrecords.com.au
HeartLand Records

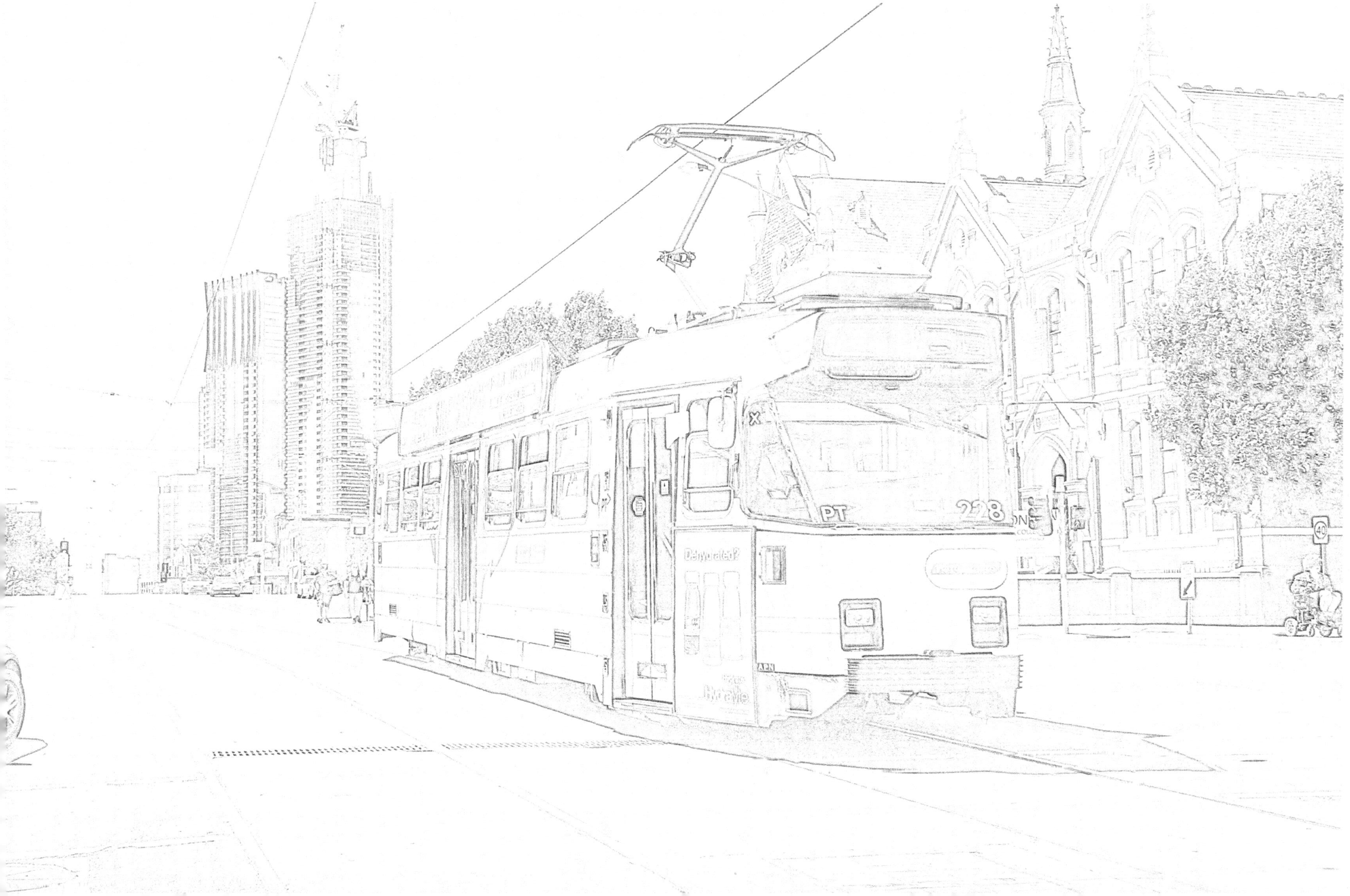
PT
228
Dehydrated?
40

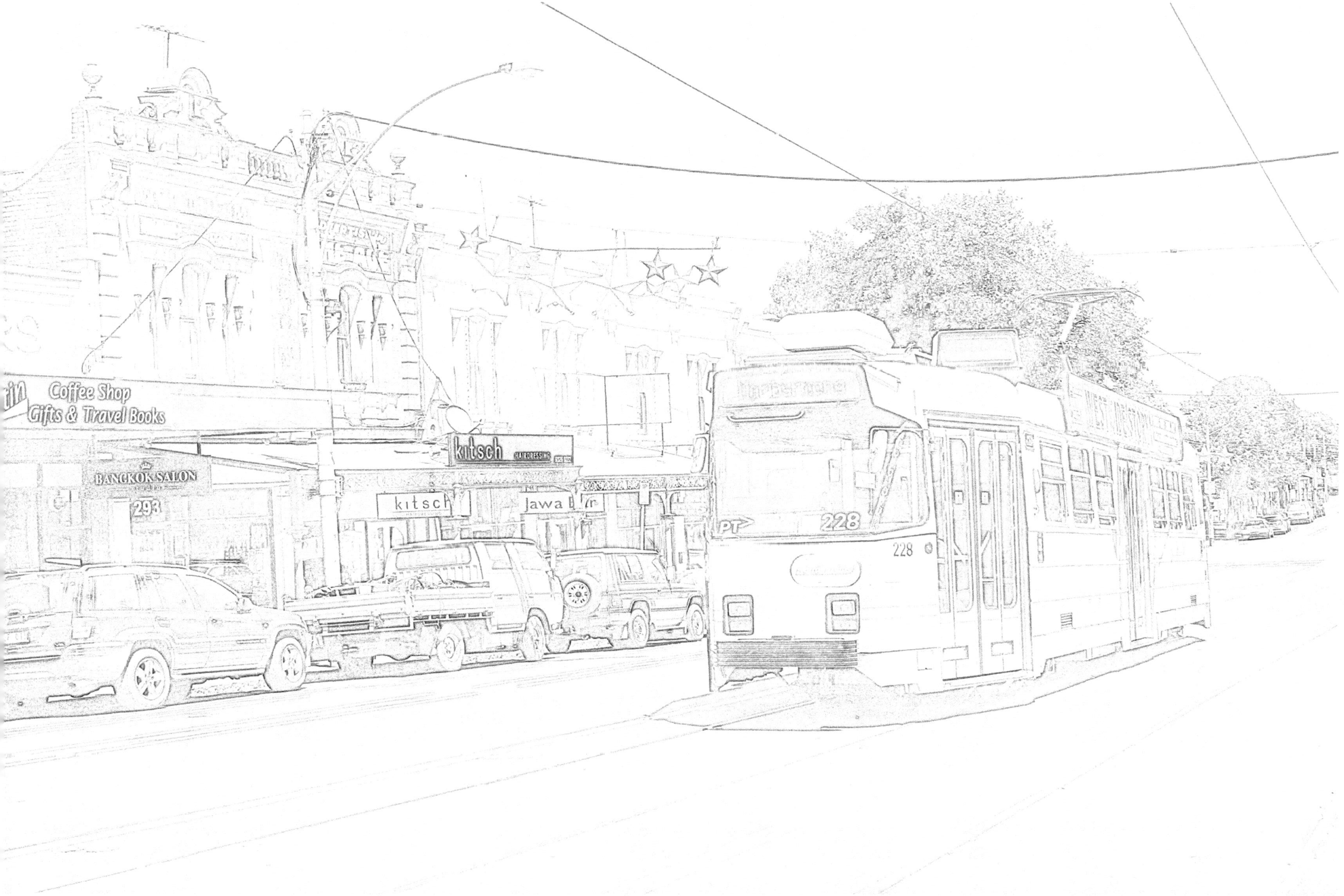

Coffee Shop
Gifts & Travel Books
BANGKOK SALON
293
kitsch
HAIRDRESSING
kitsch
PT
228
228

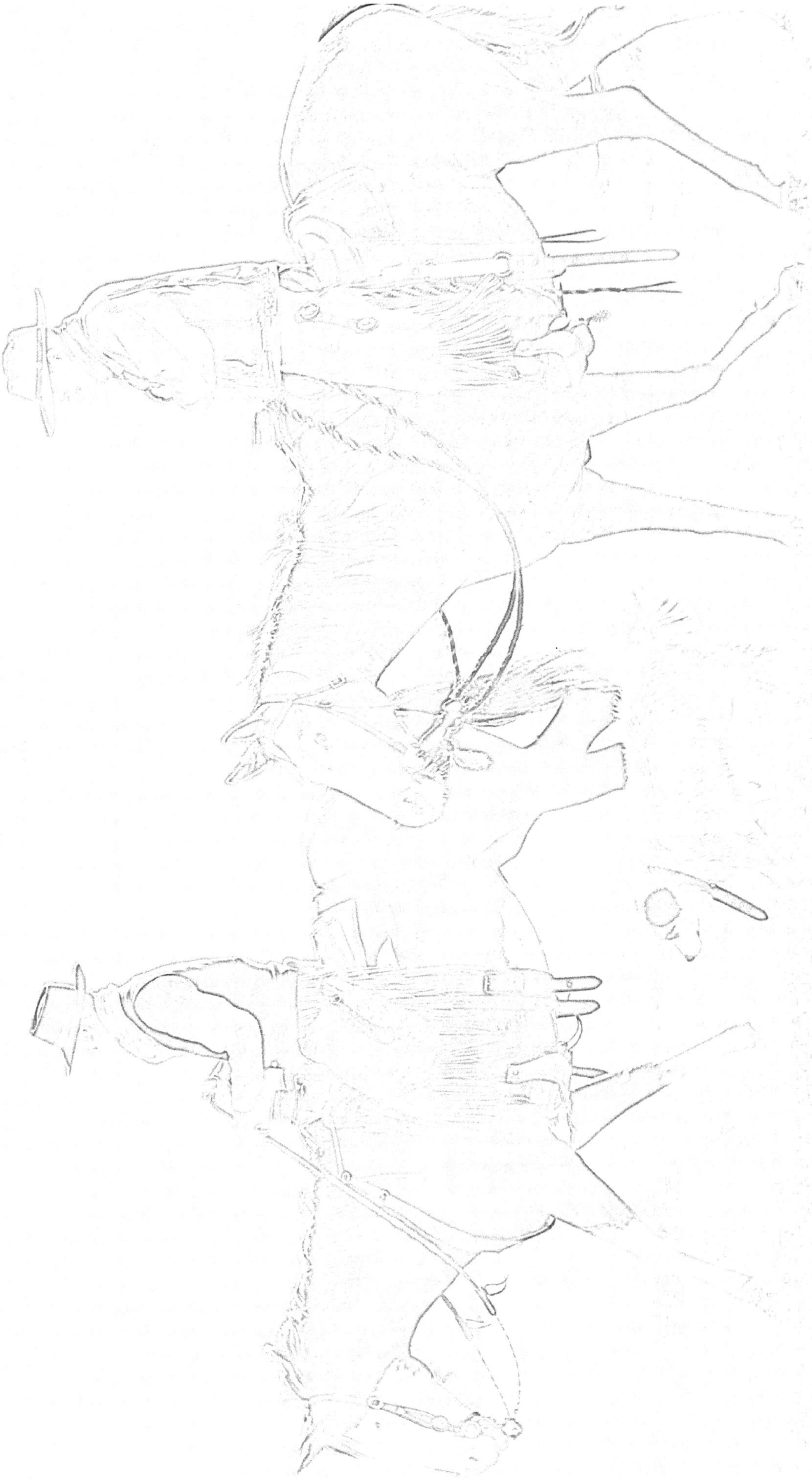

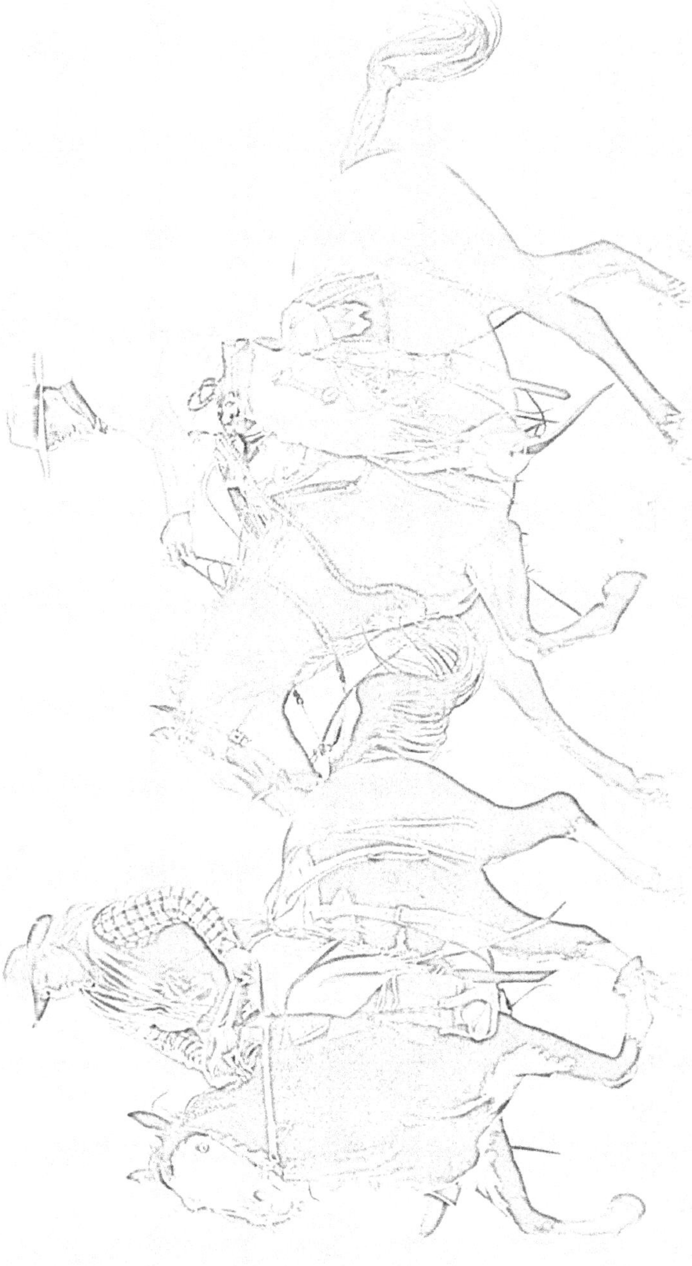

www.ingramcontent.com/pod-product-compliance
Lightning Source LLC
Chambersburg PA
CBHW081051180526
45170CB00005B/1761
9780359825165